Latina Empowerment Through Leadership

"There is immense power and courage in women of color intentionally coming together to share genuine stories of their struggles and successes at such a pivotal time in history."
—The Huffington Post

Table of Contents

INTRODUCTION

Life is made up of many moving parts— failures, successes, the good times, the bad times and all the in-between times. At each stage, our experiences teach and prepare us for transformational challenges that will shape the life we want.

As Latina women, oftentimes competing in the same arenas as men, the stakes are higher and the expectations greater. Handling it all, from the pursuit of varied passions, raising families, and assuming many responsibilities and leadership roles have an impact on our mental, emotional and physical lives.

In this book, you will meet strong and inspirational women who have been through it all... meeting challenges face-on and not only surviving, but thriving.

These remarkable women share their stories about finding balance, becoming influencers, growing into leadership, starting entrepreneurial businesses and embracing opportunities they never imagined.

Listen to them and learn from their stories about staying true to yourself and following your heart; about believing in hard work, honesty, and caring for others; about pursuing goals to never stop learning; and about utilizing technology as a powerful tool for communication.

These empowered women are the leaders of today, sharing their experiences to let others know there are no boundaries and to help current and future generations step into their own roles of leadership. These women serve as exemplary leaders in their communities, sharing the inspirations and the experiences that gave them the strength to fuel their own growth and empowerment.

As positive role models, they communicate their powerful messages through the chapters in this book. So read and get to know the importance of family, culture, diversity, innovation and education through these mindful stories from 8 inspiring women.

LESSONS LEARNED ON MY
ROAD TO LEADERSHIP

Since the day I was born, I was taught that leaders lead by example. From the moment I opened my eyes, I was surrounded by women who were empowering and did good things for others. When challenges arose, they turned them into opportunities. These women were warriors. Women, whatever challenges they came across, who never, ever gave up because of the love they had for their families, their children, and themselves. Women who valued themselves and knew they could do anything they wanted.

So, we came together and demonstrated to everyone that we never allowed ourselves to crumble. My grandmother, for example, my abuelita, was the greatest inspiration in my life, my role model. She was a warrior and was respected and loved by many. When she spoke, everybody listened. She showed kindness, love, philanthropy, and compassion to people, and, boy, did she love with passion! She loved everyone—her kids, her grandkids, her nieces, and her nephews. She taught me that no matter what, I always had to keep my head high and that I could make anything happen, as long as I believed with all my heart. But, I always had to maintain my dignity and my integrity. That is so valuable to me as a woman.

I want to show the world that everything I do has a purpose, to help someone. We are women, and we are fragile, but, at the same time, we are mothers, lawyers, doctors, nurses, drivers, and psychologists to our loved ones. That is what makes us strong, but we have to value these gifts that heaven sent—gifts that are priceless. We can't expect anyone to value that for us. As women, we have to learn to help and build up one another. We have to empower one another, strengthen one another, and help elevate one another; not find a way to hurt ourselves or destroy one another.

Growing up in a Latino home, where I saw my dad (what I call my stepdad) work really hard to build a business, was another way to see a leader in my life. My dad was a man who created a mini gold mine with his business and brought so much technology to South America. He worked hard to maintain his family and his kids and also taught me never to give up. As women, we often have important men in our lives to help us understand the sense of leadership. My dad was a wonderful man and taught me that whatever happens, I always have to get up and keep trying. Keep trying!

"Cathy, you have got to keep trying! It's okay if you have made one mistake or many. Remember, it's not how many times you fail. It's how many times you get up and try again. Are you my daughter? My daughter doesn't give up; my girl never gives up! You have a whole life ahead of you!"

His favorite saying was, "*No le pares bola*," which means "Pay no mind. Just keep going." I saw how many business deals he did, but no matter how wrong they went at times, he always found a way to locate another opportunity. He was another leader in my life who taught me that I could do anything my heart desired, as long as I didn't give up and I put passion and love into it and did it for a reason. My purpose was what kept me going.

That fire and fervor that we Latinas have will always be there, but we also have to try to keep it alive. No one can do that for us. We are the leaders of our own lives, and we have to understand that. We have to own it. *Es parte de ser Latina y es parte de ser mujer. Esa pasión que tenemos cuando reímos y cuando hablamos*—when we laugh, when we cry, when we speak, when we love our children, when we love our spouses or partners, and when we love our friends and our families. We are passionate in everything we do. It is part of who we are.

My father (what I call my biological father) was a man of integrity and honor, an amazing man with an incredible heart. He was also big on loyalty and honesty. He was a man who would walk away from anything that would put his credibility in doubt. He was also another leader in my life. I respected him and loved him dearly from afar. He taught me that honesty is the most important thing that we have. Also, our integrity is important toward what we do, our businesses, our clients, our families, our friends, and to everyone who is part of our lives. He inspired me to always live up to that. I always made sure to make him proud, because that's how he raised his children, with honesty and with trust, which is something that we must have as part of our leadership skills and our life.

Those are steps that we have to follow to be respected in our communities, to love our communities, and to be followed by our communities. That is how leaders are made. They are made by who looks up to them and who respects them. With a leader, it is never, "Do as I say." It is always, "Do as I do." Once again, we lead by example.

How can I forget one of the most influential leaders in my life—my mother? My beautiful mother! A lady in every sense of the word, *una dama*. She was a woman who carried herself with such respect, so much love, and so much class. No one can ever point at my mother and judge her. People love her and respect her for the kindness of her heart. Boy, was she hard on me growing up, and I never understood why. However, today I thank her for that. I am the woman I am because of her leadership and because of what I saw in her.

She was the one who most of the time told me, "*Tú puedes!* Clean your tears; go get it. *Tú puedes!* Don't cry; you got this. Why do you weep? Do you think you are lesser? Don't cry. Get up and do it. I know you can do it. Why do you doubt yourself?"

My mother was a woman who always believed in me, and I get to see it today. I realize that she was more of a leader in my life than anybody else was. My mother and my grandmother influenced my life in many ways. Leaders do lead by example. However, they also make mistakes, and they are not always perfect.

At age 22, I encountered the separation of my dad and my mom and the loss of everything. Coming from private schools and a good life, my mom, my siblings, and I were forced to switch our pattern of life. We had to learn to overcome all these struggles and figure things out on our own, because we were never taught differently. We were never prepared, but we learned with time and by sticking together as a *familia*. I promised myself that I would never be in that position again. However, that was not possible.

Years later, I got married and had three beautiful children, whom I'm extremely proud of. My ex-husband and I had a successful business, a great life, and a beautiful home. When the market crashed in 2007, we lost everything. There I was, again, in the same position that I had been in 10 years earlier. However, I did learn from my previous experience and had something set aside in case of a "rainy day." I protected my kids, and I protected my family. At that moment of loss, my ex-husband realized how important it was that we had something set aside for a "rainy day."

One day I woke up, and it clicked, "What? Wait! That's it, oh my God. Yes!" I realized that I had found a passion in my heart, a passion for educating the Latino community on the importance of life insurance, retirement planning, and protecting their futures.

As Latinos, we work hard to achieve our dreams and our goals. We build dreams for others, and we build dreams for ourselves. We take pride in everything we do, but we don't know how to protect what we worked so hard for. It's not part of our culture. I decided that I would be that empowering Latina who teaches my community the importance of protecting the ones they love.

Today, I'm so proud of what I've done, of how many women I've taught, how many children I've educated, how many universities I've spoken at, how many people are protected, and how many people have learned to protect the ones they love. These parents became leaders to their own families and to their loved ones. Women have learned to achieve their own successful retirements and dreams. I have empowered people to become their own leaders and to have their own financial independence. I think, as a leader, I have made an impact on my community. Therefore, I will continue to lead my Latino community by example.

And this is where the challenge came. I thought, *How do I reach out to a community that, for the most part, has no understanding of the importance of life insurance and retirement planning?* Most of them don't understand the significance of it. That's when I realized that everything had to be based on trust. Before anything, I had to show my community that I wanted to do what was best for them. They needed to see my actions and what I did before they could trust me. So, I got involved in many organizations: chambers of commerce, community events, philanthropies, fundraisers, schools, and I provided financial literacy workshops, in which I gave information to my community (in Spanish) about how important it was to plan for the future.

It was challenging in the beginning, once I told people what I wanted to do. Some of them smirked at me, and some of them laughed at me. They would look at me and say, "Latinos? Life insurance? Ha! Good luck with that. You're gonna starve. Latinos don't understand that. They don't want to hear it! They would rather sell food and do fundraisers to raise enough money to bury their loved ones.

I thought for a moment, *This is why, even as a strong community that provides so much for the economy, we are not respected! We fall back on the most important things that will show others that not only do we work hard, but we are also prepared.* Sadly, it's true, we work hard to provide for our families, and we think we're protecting our loved ones in the best way possible, but we aren't.

It took time, but I let my people know. I told them, "Do you want to be respected and do things in this country that are valuable? Or do you want to be the one to put your family through the pain of doing everything possible to collect enough money to bury you? I think you want to be buried with dignity and not leave your family ashamed. That's why it is important that you plan, because you never know what might come tomorrow." I realized that people were right. It was going to be hard, but the more they told me I couldn't do it, the more I remembered the leaders in my family.

I thought about my dad and when he told me to never to give up, to ignore when things were hard and just keep going. I also remembered my father telling me that I had to do things with integrity and honesty. Then, I remembered my mother telling me to wipe my tears and keep going no matter how many people tried to put me down. I was laughed at, people mocked me, people rolled their eyes at me, and many times people thought that I was going to try to get things because of the way

I looked. That was so offensive to me, because I figured they doubted my intelligence and integrity to my community. My grandmother came to mind, and I remembered her saying, "If you do it with love, and you show others what you're trying to do before you ask, they're going to know how trustworthy you are and come to you."

All these leaders in my life helped me make such an impact on my community. So, I started to implement everything I learned from them. I reached out to many community leaders, who today I have a strong relationship with. They trust me, they know what I'm doing for my community, and, most important, they believe in my vision. I build relationships with people who I know understand me, who trust me, based on what I've shown them, and how I handle myself in front of my community as a woman of respect.

I still remember the times I went to visit families and they invited me for dinner. They shared stories of how they came to this country—their dreams, their expectations, and everything they wanted to achieve. After they shared, it was my turn to speak. I asked them how they were going to protect themselves and their families and how they were going to prepare for the unexpected. It was my time to educate them, based on what they shared with me.

That's how my culture is. We're about sharing stories, and that's exactly what I did. I shared my story. I told them about the time that my family, my siblings, my mother, and I went through a big struggle. I also educated many women and families about this matter, and I showed them how important it is that they protect their families, so they could prevent themselves from going through the hardships that I went through. How could they possibly not want to educate themselves and risk doing this to their children and families? I told them the story of when I lost everything and my kids suffered because of it.

My story became a message to my Latino community. I wanted them to understand the importance of planning for their futures. That's when I realized I was on the right path. I realized that nothing could stop me, and all I had to do was keep going and pushing, because I had friends and people who supported me and believed in everything that I said. Although there were women at the beginning who tried really hard to make me crumble, I did not let them. It saddened me to see how some women could be so destructive. As I mentioned before, we need to build up one another, we need to elevate one another, NOT destroy one another! So, I kept my chin up and kept going. I formed alliances with women who motivated one another and had the same vision I did, which was to help our Latino communities. They were Latinas who were leaders, mothers, entrepreneurs, and who understood that what I was trying to do for my community was the same as what they were trying to do with their businesses. That made me stronger.

There were nights I'd come home and look at my kids and think, *One day, when I am no longer here, I want my kids to remember what I did for our community, the memories that I left, and my legacy."* I want them to remember what I showed and what I taught our community. Their mother was making an impact, and they were going to be able to be so proud of me because of what I had done. It's not only what I can leave them financially, but also how they're going to feel, knowing that I took the time to focus on our community and teach others the importance of planning to protect their loved ones. I wanted to make sure that other mothers would protect themselves from going through what I went through.

If my kids only knew how much strength they gave me.

At times, I would watch them sleep and say, "We went through it once, and I'm trying so hard for you not to feel my struggles." I would walk into their rooms, lean in, and watch them sleep, knowing that they were the ones who inspired me the most at that time. That Latina mother, driver, and empowering woman was coming out of me more often, because my kids gave me the strength and motivation to keep going.

I loved to hear them tell me how proud they were every time they saw me give a speech or a presentation; to see my daughter with that smile on her face, because she knew that her mom was trying to make an impact and a difference; to have my son give me a hug and tell me how proud he was of me; and to have my little one say, "Hey, Mama, are you doing all these things for these families? Are you protecting their futures, Mom? That's awesome. How do you do that?" It's just so uplifting. I was already planting a seed within my kids, without even knowing. My children became my incentive.

There was no turning back, because I knew I was onto something. I was making a change. You can call me an activist, call me outspoken, call me whatever you want. When it comes to judging me, because of how I want to get in front of community leaders who I know will understand what I'm trying to do, I don't care. Because I know what I'm doing is for a good cause, and I want to be a voice for my community.

I am so grateful for how much I have achieved, and how much I will be able to achieve in many aspects of my career. I am able to help organizations and do philanthropic work, which is something I am so passionate about because of my grandmother and my mother. They always taught me that no matter how much someone hurts you or tries to deceive you, keep going and don't ever let it change your heart and the way you feel about the world! It fills me with gratification that I know I have become the person that my community comes to for information and advice.

It was hard being labeled as just "another insurance agent," and it was heartbreaking to see how many insurance agents have taken advantage of my fellow Latinos, who thought that they had a good life insurance product or a good retirement plan. But in the end, they'd come to see that they had been mis-sold and misled. It was heartbreaking for me to see that our own people were being taken advantage of, so I decided that needed to stop. If we don't help one another, then nobody's going to help us, especially in this time we live in.

So, I remembered that I had another story to tell. It was about my family being taken advantage of by Latinos in the life insurance world. I grew up with my grandparents in Ecuador for the first 12 years of my life. We moved back to New York, so I could start high school and later college. I was a senior in high school, when my grandfather decided that he wanted to write his will. He explained to me how he was going to write it and put it on paper. To be honest, I didn't want anything to do with it, because I didn't have the best relationship with most of his children from his first marriage, and I did not want to be part of that negative energy. So, I asked him to please not include me in the will.

That's when the idea came to him to leave me a life insurance policy. He called a life insurance agent and asked for the same value of his will to be in a life insurance policy. For about 20 years, my grandfather paid for his insurance policy, but at the time of his death, I was not able to claim it. Not only did I have to go through the pain of losing my grandfather, who was like a father in my heart, but I had to encounter that he had been lied to for so many years by someone who had no heart, no loyalty, and no rectitude toward his clients. It was utterly heartbreaking for me.

Now I had another story to tell my clients so they could understand that they needed to learn and educate themselves on everything they have and everything they buy. It is crucial for all our communities to be educated and informed, not misled like my grandfather was.

The worst part in this situation is that many Latinos are taking advantage of other Latinos. As one of my close friends began to read the life insurance policy to me, I realized that my grandfather had purchased a policy that protected me *only* if he had died from a car accident. I had no knowledge then about what kind of policy he had. Memories came to my head of when we would sit down and enjoy dinner or a walk through New York City, and he would remind me of his life insurance policy for me so that I could be taken care of. We would crack jokes about it and how I was going to donate it to some poor family. He would laugh about it and say, "I wouldn't doubt it." My grandfather and I had such an amazing relationship; my grandparents made my childhood so memorable and beautiful.

Ultimately, I think that was the hardest part—that someone who so loved his family was cheated and lied to. It wasn't the value of the life insurance policy that mattered. It was that for years, my grandfather thought that the day he was not going to be here, there was going to be something there for me, in case I ever needed it. All I can say is that the day I found out, I sat and prayed to my grandfather to one day bless me and help me build something that would be equal to or greater than whatever he left me. I think that is one of the reasons that I feel so much passion in my heart to help my community. Though I had great leaders in my life, they were also misinformed and didn't take the time to inform and educate themselves about something so important.

It made me happy to know my grandfather tried and thought he was protecting me. That's why I had to do something about it. I was going to be working with people, in my grandfather's honor, and give my community the right information. It came to the point where I would sit with clients and show them what was wrong with their policies, and they were so surprised. I also gave them a list of questions they should ask their agents. It is sad to say that many times I was right, and I had to hear the saddening news of them being cheated. It was shocking that many times I would sit with Latino families to plan for their children's future and often their multiple concerns were to save for their daughter's quinceñera instead of her college education.

At that moment, I realized that I had to speak in a way that people would understand. Latinos love to spend money and are often compulsive buyers, and I concluded that I needed to make sure that I always asked the right questions. Based on my training I knew the perfect question, the home run, was, "What day of the week do you spend the most money?" The answer was usually Sunday, to which I replied, "Well, when you retire, every day will be a Sunday. Are you ready for that?" This is when they finally processed my reply, and they became more eager to hear about it. That's when I knew I had delivered my message.

We have to come together as women and men in the Latino community and become a team, a *familia*. We need to become a union that is based on our foods, our beliefs, and our traditions. Regardless of the diversity of our cultures, we communicate in one language, and that language should bring us together. We have to do it in the most positive way possible, if we want to educate our future leaders, our children, who will be involved with this country. Parents need to understand that their children watch everything they do and that they need to lead by example.

Financial literacy is key, not only for our Latino community. This concept should be taught in all schools from an early age. This knowledge would prevent so much hardship for our new generations and our future leaders. It would be a good way to maintain many businesses and prevent failures. It would also be a way to release families from their financial burdens.

As for our Latino community, we need to make financial literacy the most important part of our growth in future planning. We are a big asset to this country and need to focus on educating ourselves; we are hard workers with strength of passion and perseverance. Latinos are a perfect example of why we come to this country.

We want to show others that the sky is not the limit—there is always the universe.

CATHERINE GARCES

Catherine was born in New York City, but at a very young age moved to Ecuador and was raised by her grandparents.  When she turned 14 years old moved back to the United States where Catherine finished her studies and later received her degree in Hotel & Restaurant Management. During her years attending High School, she was involved with the student government program, which allowed her to share ideas once a month, with the Senator of New York, Mr. Maltese. Right after college, a scholarship to attend Cornell University and an offer to work an internship program with Donald Trump came, however she declined and started her career in the hotel industry at a corporate level.

When Catherine was 16 years old, her dad owned an Importing/Exporting company and in her spare time would learn the International Business World. After a few years of learning from her father she decided that type of business was not for her. At that same time, she witnessed her father's growing business take a deep fall due to lack of knowledge in financial planning. This is what motivated Catherine to get on this journey of educating on the importance of Life insurance, retirement planning, and how to protect your business, and due to her cultural background she decided to focus in the Latino community.

From here on, her life took a 180 degree turn and she became an inspiration to both men and women in the community.

She was featured on several magazines as a woman creating awareness.

Was awarded Ambassador of the Year for the Orange County Hispanic Chamber of Commerce.

Catherine has planned and participated in multiple philanthropic events in Los Angeles and Orange County.

Has received recognitions from Congress, Mayors from several cities in California and from the Police department in Los Angeles due to her committed work during her corporate position in New York Life.

Worked with over 20 YMCAs across LA providing the Child ID program (Safety for Kids).

She is very actively involved and supports several non-profit organizations: LatinaVIDA. Kids with Autism. Woman Health and Wealth among many others.

Catherine continues to be invited as a guest speaker to various Schools, Universities, Radio, Television and different panels of Social Media to speak about financial planning and overcoming adversities.

She is also known as a big influencer, philanthropist and leader in the Latino community.

One of Catherine's major strengths in life is her faith in God.

MUJER, CHINGONA, PODEROSA—

THIS IS FOR YOU

You are not a statistic. You are not a sex object meant to be eroticized. You are powerful beyond measure, and I am here to lift you up. So pour yourself a *cafecito* or shot of tequila, take a seat and come journey with me through my fears, missteps, breakdowns and finally, my successes.

Con Amor,
Monica Rivera

SEVENTEEN

"Did you hear about the rose that grew / from a crack in the concrete? / Proving nature's law is wrong / it learned to walk without having feet. / Funny it seems, but by keeping its dreams, / it learned to breathe fresh air. / Long live the rose that grew from concrete / when no one else ever cared." —Tupac Shakur

Her hand was soft, fragile in mine and I could see the purple black blossoming under her thin skin where the nurses had poked her one too many times. I remember her telling me, "Mija, I love you" and knowing we were close to the end. *I was seventeen years old when my grandmother passed away.*

I'm the youngest of six, and the only one from both parents, blessed with a safe home and an opportunity to attend a private school when my siblings weren't so lucky. I grew up around gangs, drugs and alcoholism. I've visited more prisons than I can count, palms pressed against the cold glass, wishing only for the warmth of his hug. *I was seventeen years old when my brother was sentenced to three years, his longest so far, and I realized he'd miss my high school graduation.*

Straight-A, honors student, in drama club and choir and student council, volunteering in convalescent homes in my spare time... the perfect picture of a 'good kid.' Binge drinking on the weekends in the hills of Whitter and getting blackout drunk, sobering up enough by the time I got home so my parents would never know. *I was seventeen years old when I was sexually assaulted.*

I fell into depression. Have you ever been underwater for just a little too long? The pressure pushing in from all sides, and the more you struggle, the more disoriented you become. Your stomach in knots, heart beating fast, not knowing left and right from up and down, and being pulled further and further into the darkness. Waves pounding down, and just when you get your head out of the water for a minute, another comes crashing down. *I was seventeen years old when I started using cocaine to make that feeling go away.*

Seventeen.

The year I started applying to colleges, went on my first date, had my first romantic kiss... the year I lost my grandmother and myself... the year I had bruises on my thighs reminding me of whose hands had been there.... The year I fell into a despair so deep without ever batting an eyelash.... without ever letting anyone else know.

Seventeen. **The year I survived.**

I don't say these things for you to feel sorry for me. I say them so you know where I've been, what I've made it through, so you know that YOU can make it through, too.

The circumstances of our lives aren't something that we can change. There are things that happen to you and to me, and there's no getting around that. But the decisions I made as a result, the good and the bad, those were mine. I was never "powerless" over my choices and there is no one to blame but me.

Every single day, we make powerful decisions that impact our lives. Knowing that, understanding and acknowledging it, THAT is the beginning of self-leadership. It's the ability to have awareness of one's own character, feelings, strengths and faults and to act on them... because if I had the power to make those decisions, then I too, had the power to make new ones.

> "You don't drown by falling in water. You drown by staying there." — Ed Cole

And though it took some time, I refused to drown.

TURNING POINT

> "There is only one thing that makes a dream impossible to achieve: the fear of failure." — Paulo Coelho, The Alchemist

That same year, I sat outside on a sunny day waiting to be called into the guidance counselor's office for feedback on my college applications. I was looking down, hands shaky, palms clammy, when he finally called me in.

What happened in those next ten minutes changed my life. I figured going into that room, he'd look over my essays, check my letters of recommendation and give me advice to improve. After all, guidance counselors are supposed to guide, right?

I remember sitting across from him at this big oak desk, listening to the ticking of the clock as the hands slowly dragged on. My fingernails dug in as I gripped the cushion of the chair I was sitting on, where I'm sure countless other nails had dug in before. I could smell pencil shavings and the salt of the cold sweat forming on my brow, my mouth dry like a desert, and my left leg shaking a mile a minute. Waiting. Just waiting.

Finally, he tossed my essays and letters to the side, scanned my list of potential schools, looked me dead in the eye and said, "Don't bother applying to The University of Southern California. You won't get in."

At that moment, my heart pounded, and the blood rushed into my ears. I could have thrown in the towel. I could have accepted what he said as truth. But I didn't.

Change can happen in a single instance with one single decision, and that was the moment I made mine. Perhaps it was the year I had just experienced or the voice in my head from my strong-willed mother who takes no one's shit. Maybe I was just tired of hurting, or maybe it was a combination of all of that... but the next two words that rolled off my tongue surprised even me,

"Watch Me."

Soy chingona y bien cabrona tambien and the desire to prove him wrong ran deeper than my despair. It was a turning point in my life, and as angry as I was at that moment, I will be forever grateful.

You see, what you focus on with emotion and belief, you will attract into your life, and I became incredibly focused. I made the decision to prove him wrong, and in doing so, I set a powerful and clear goal for myself. My pain was replaced with a hunger for more. The depression, with a belief in myself and my potential. I began cultivating the mindset of leadership and gained confidence in my own ability to dictate my future.

Can you think back now to a time when someone told you that you couldn't do something? Did you believe them? Did you accept that as your new truth? What did you start telling yourself as a result?

Our words and our beliefs have immense power over our lives, both negative and positive. When someone tells you that you can't do something and you accept it as truth, you form limiting beliefs. This instills fear and self-doubt and becomes a self-fulfilling prophecy of failure.

But that's not living. No one but you can define your limitations, so don't let someone else's words dilute your magic. Be mindful about what you project into the universe.

Mahatma Gandhi once said, *"Your beliefs become your thoughts, your thoughts become your words, your words become your actions, your actions become your habits, your habits become your values, your values become your destiny."* So, become intentional about your thoughts and self-talk. Believe in yourself. You are capable of more than you know.

And by the way, I was accepted to and attended USC.

PASSION

"You cannot raise a child like a lion and expect her to become
a sheep because society feels she must follow the path of her
peers." — Ijeoma Umebinyuo

In college, I truly thought I had my life all figured out. I was riding something I like to call the 'Elevator Model of Success.' It looks a little something like this:

1.   Pick a career trajectory and hop on the elevator.

2.   Do well in school.

3.   Go to college and get a degree in a major that aligns with that career.

4.   Work at all the right internships.

5.   Graduate.

6.   Get an entry-level position.

7.   Ride the elevator up, behind a line of people doing *the same damn thing*, until they step off at retirement and you get a promotion!

8.   Until finally, **ding** the doors open and you step off for your own retirement.

That's exactly the path I intended to follow. I started as a Psychology major with a Pre-law emphasis. I was obsessed with the tv show <u>Law & Order</u> while I was growing up and decided I'd ride the elevator all the way to law school and become a Forensic Psychologist.

Thankfully, that lasted less than a week. My first day of Psych 101, as I listened to the professor ramble on about the syllabus, I realized there was no way in hell I was going to do this for the rest of my life. The problem is, the 'Elevator Model' is based on the societal expectation of what we think we're supposed to do rather than how we want to feel. It lacks passion and purpose, and although Forensic Psychologist might be an incredible career choice for some, it didn't light me up inside.

And so, I exited stage left. I was THAT girl, saying *"excuse me, pardon me"* in the middle of a jam-packed class as I rushed to get out. I dropped the class, dropped my major, became 'undeclared' and didn't tell my parents for a year.

But for the first time, there weren't enough hours in the day. I took classes on Hip Hop, Gang Intervention, The Meaning of Life and Business. Those classes lit my soul on fire. Days flew by. It was like working on a puzzle, and the picture was finally starting to form. I was inspired, alive and finally letting my passion take the lead.

Those passions manifested in 2010 when, inspired by the various subjects I had studied, I founded <u>Bless My Hustle</u> as a blog looking at success through the lens of hip-hop and pop culture. My goal was to empower others to get off the elevator and create their own success, no matter how untraditional their paths might be, but it became so much more.

Because the project came from a place of passion, it allowed me to speak confidently, articulately and with self-assurance in my voice and people were attracted to that. Without trying, my passion had commanded attention and inspired people to follow me. The phrase had soon traveled all around the world, including Africa and Dubai, through the blog and the hundreds of wristbands I gave away. It caught media attention and was the reason I got a chance to work on a project with Will.I.Am. and Nasa back in 2011 and to share a stage with Kevin Harrington of ABC's Shark Tank in 2014.

It was a valuable lesson on leadership and on the magnetism that comes from exploring that which you love.

What do you love? What passions light you up and make you crave more? How can you pursue that in some way, shape, or form?

Make it a priority to find your fire. Passions give you depth and inspire commitment, dedication and hard work for yourself and your life. When you lead with passion and speak from your soul, you don't have to chase people or opportunities. You become magnetic to those opportunities. Take advantage of that.

For me, it was just the beginning of understanding the power of my voice and learning to take advantage of the open doors that were put in my path, whether they fell into what was traditionally acceptable or not. But I still had a lot to learn.

CLOSING A DOOR

"I've put up with too much, too long, and now I'm just too intelligent, too powerful, too beautiful, too sure of who I am finally to deserve anything less." —Sandra Cisneros

While at USC, I refused to ask my parents for money because I knew they had sacrificed so much to get me there, something I will be forever grateful for. Instead, I worked multiple jobs over my years as a student.

I worked my way through the Real Estate industry in property management. And I fell in love with marketing at a time when social media was just starting to take off and spent time as a Marketing Director in the consumer products industry managing brands like Jarritos® and Del Real Foods®. I also got into the Online Community Management space and managed teams upwards of 15 people while overseeing social engagement for one of the top collegiate digital publications in the nation.

Each of those experiences was beyond amazing, but life is short. And it can become a whole lot shorter when you spend your days dealing with a bad boss. I had not one, but two bad bosses.

I'm a big believer that things like alcohol and money and power don't change you; they enhance who you already are. And these were just not good people. Rather than helping their employees grow and evolve, they let the power of leadership go to their heads. Instead of reprimanding employees for simple mistakes behind closed doors or providing constructive criticism and feedback, I heard them scream and shout using words like *stupid, idiot* and even worse, *wetback.*

The thing is, you can't control the behavior of others. You can only control your reaction to that behavior. Often, we convince ourselves that we have no other options, but the truth is we have a choice. I could have stayed silent, becoming a bystander to injustice until that same negativity was turned towards me. Or, I could respect myself and my team enough to speak out and leave.

And so, there I was going to school and work every day, loving my co-workers, loving the office. And yet, I found myself in these situations where I was grinding my teeth, my fists clenched. I had this humming feeling of being coiled too tightly underneath skin and sinew and bone that I steadily ignored... until I couldn't ignore it anymore.

Have you ever had a similar experience? Be it a bad situation, an unfulfilling job, unsupportive friends, a painful relationship?

You can choose to stay in those soul-crushing environments and complain about your life. You can choose to wish things were better and hope they'll change. Or you can lead with your own integrity and truth and choose to be that change. Respect yourself enough to walk away from those things that no longer serve you, because you determine your worth by how you let people treat you. And when you find yourself in a position of leadership, remember what it is to be on the other side.

My choice? I closed a door. No, not closed, I slammed a door. I dead-bolted it, threw away the key, and then I turned around, hammered it shut for good measure and hung an 'I quit' sign in the window.

GROWTH

"For a seed to achieve its greatest expression, it must come
completely undone. The shell cracks, its insides come out,
and everything changes. To someone who doesn't understand
growth, it would look like complete destruction." —Cynthia Occelli

The next few years were rough. I had decided to pursue entrepreneurship
and went through my fair share of failures and successes. At one point, I
lived out of a suitcase in the back room of my very first real office, where
I slept on a blow-up air mattress that would deflate halfway through each
night. I guess you could say I was a "cereal" entrepreneur, because since
I put all my money back into the business and personal development, I
lived on 33 cent Maruchan® Ramen and cereal for months on end.

In reality, that was one of the best decisions I ever could have made.
Despite the long days, sleepless nights, empty bank accounts, empty
refrigerators and the many, many failures, it was my commitment to
learning on which I saw the biggest return.

After countless business seminars, professional coaching programs and
finally gaining focus and clarity, I shut the door on my many ventures
to focus on a property management company I had started with two
friends. By the end of our first year, we'd doubled our business, hired our
first employee and negotiated a merger with a company we had consulted for
before. We set a three-year goal which we hit in six months, hired a staff of 14
and by the time I left, just another year later, we'd hit seven figure revenue.
But it sounds a lot more glamorous than it was.

Although business growth is desirable and exciting, when it happens too quickly, it can lead to serious problems. In the end, the egos, the drama, the broken friendships— they weren't worth it for me, and I decided to walk away.

I've walked away from destructive situations before, but somehow this was different, and so much worse. The day I signed my stake in the company away, check in hand, I drove straight to my parents' house. I spent the 45-minute car ride going back and forth between heart-wrenching sobs and hysterical laughter. That's the thing about birthing something from your own blood, sweat and tears— it becomes your baby, a part of you, and it feels like an incredible, heartbreaking loss when you let go.

It was the first time in my adult life that I had a blank slate in front of me, and it terrified me.

But the countless investments in my personal development, the knowledge and business acumen, those aren't things that can be taken away. My mind had stretched and it wasn't going back. And I had gained incredible resilience. The blank slate before me was an opportunity.

The truth is, you must always invest in yourself and your growth. It pays the best interest. Because when things begin to fall apart and you lose everything you've built, the education, knowledge and leadership skills you've gained will stay with you for the rest of your life. And you can start again.

LEGACY

"In the end, she became more than what she expected. She became the journey, and like all journeys, she did not end, she just simply changed directions and kept going." —R.M. Drake

A week later, my paternal grandmother was admitted to the hospital. When released, she was no longer able to be on her own, and because

I suddenly had no work commitments and endless time on my hands, I could be there for her.

I spent the next four months caring for her. We'd cook traditional dishes like *pipian* and *mole*, me doing the work and her instructing and tasting. We'd watch *telenovelas*, discuss politics and listen to music. And we'd sit outside where she'd tell me stories about her youth, her many suitors and their *serenatas*, falling in love with my grandfather and finally leaving Mexico. There was one particular story that awoke something in me.

My grandmother, a mother of six, followed her husband to California where they both worked in factories and saved up the money they needed to build a home for their family and bring the children they had left behind to the land of opportunity. Together they created a home, but rather than the quintessential dream home with the white picket fence, they purchased a three-unit property where they could start to plant their own roots, build a home and create a legacy.

As she told me this story for the first time, her story, she said, *"Hay que sembrar para cosechar."* You have to plant the seeds in order to reap the harvest.

That little three-unit property takes care of her until this day. It's the reason my dad became a real estate investor planting his own seeds and investing in assets. It's the reason that as a little girl, he took me with him to see the apartments and homes he and my mother had bought and rented out, filled with *orgullo* at the legacy that they were building one home at a time. It's why when he taught me to drive at the age of seventeen, I learned to change lanes while we drove from home auction to home auction, learning so much more than I ever could have hoped to pick up in Drivers Ed.

THAT was her harvest, her legacy. Not just a property to take care of her, but the beliefs and values she passed down to her family, leading so many of us to plant seeds of our own.

And that's what I wanted to create— my own legacy. That night, I sat down to think about what else I wanted, what I truly wanted, and I wrote myself a love letter.

I believe that you should be relentless when it comes to setting your soul on fire and creating the life of your dreams, but to do that, first you need clarity. You must know what you want and what you need to do to get it. You have to know how you want to feel and how to create those feelings in your life.

In the midst of working so hard to build something I didn't even love anymore, I'd forgotten that. And so I started to ask myself questions that mattered, questions you should ask yourself...

What kind of relationship did I want with my family? Was I happy with my health? Where did I want to be in a year when it came to my career? Did I want to date? Should I explore my faith? What kind of people did I want in my life?

As I answered those questions and more, my life vision started to form, and I wrote pages upon pages to myself as though I was already living the life I had imagined.

How I'd wake up every day and live passionately and without apology. That I'd look in the mirror and see someone I'm proud of. That I'd surround myself with people who speak life into my future and want to see me grow. That, inspired by my grandmother, I'd build a career around leading people, especially women, to create their own legacies by investing in themselves and investing in real estate. That I'd lead with my passion, purpose, heart and soul.

When I was done, I was left with an eight-page love letter to myself filled with goals for my future and so much emotion. I started to read it to myself every single day, and like so many years before, because I was focusing on my desires for the future and nurturing the seeds I had planted throughout my life, those desires started to manifest.

YOUR TURN

Remembering the pain, the struggle, isn't always easy. This is one of the hardest things I've ever done, putting pen to paper and letting my heart bleed. Baring my soul for you, but also for me. I'm not perfect. I've made mistakes. I've fallen into the dark waters and refused to drown. I will never be one of those well-behaved women. *Soy chingona y bien cabrona tambien* and I've been through too much darkness to dim my light.

But that's the thing—you don't have to be perfect to inspire others. People get inspired by how you deal with your own imperfections. They want your passion, your fire. And as women with struggles, we are forged from the fire.

John Quincy Adams once said, *"If your actions inspire others to dream more, learn more, do more, and become more, you are a leader."* So if I have inspired you in any of those things, then I've done my job, because leadership doesn't always mean being the head of an organization or holding a position of power. It's about one life influencing another.

If you learn only one thing from me, learn this. Fall in love with yourself and your scars, learn to follow your *corazon*, break the chains of tradition, and have *respeto* but never at the cost of your own self-respect. Know that sometimes leadership is born out of struggle, and when your passion and purpose come together, magic happens. Dream big, hustle hard, figure out your purpose and then go out and change the world. You have to be the architect of your own life plan because no one else is going to do that for you. To manifest your desires, give them attention, intent and emotion. Lead with your heart to decide what you want, what seeds you need to plant. Make a plan. Write it down. And work on it every single day. And when you doubt yourself, remember everything you've been through and overcome and keep on going. The journey isn't always easy, but trust me, it is always worth it.

MONICA RIVERA

Monica Rivera is a Realtor®, Author, Speaker and Investor who sells real estate in the greater Los Angeles area and is passionate about helping others create multi-generational wealth and influence. She has shared the stage with Kevin Harrington of ABC's Shark Tank and has been featured on multiple media outlets including Real Estate Game Changers Radio, Bustle, Realtor.com, Latino Radio, Behind The Hustle and Clarity FM.

When Monica first decided to pursue entrepreneurship, she had her fair share of struggle– at one point living out of a suit case in the back room of her first office (*on a blow-up air mattress that would deflate halfway through each night!*), before she achieved success.

After consulting for and building several successful businesses in various niches (real estate, fashion, consumer products, etc.), one of which hit 6 figures in just under 6 months, she refocused on what she loves most– making investing and wealth-building opportunities more accessible to communities of color.

As a strong believer that *"sometimes saving money and planting roots is an act of revolution"*, she is especially invested in empowering women to create multi-generational wealth by investing in themselves and in real estate.

Monica writes and speaks on the intersections of culture, wealth-building, real estate and politics and is a regular contributor to The Huffington Post, invited by Arianna Huffington herself. She is also author of **The Chingona Manifesto**™ and an investor in several tech and service based start-ups focused on serving Latinx audiences.

As a Business Success Coach and Nero linguistic Programming Master Practitioner, certified by the International Business and Entrepreneurship Association, Monica has been invited to speak and lead workshops on topics ranging from motivation and networking to branding and business at multiple collegiate institutions and national organizations, including her alma mater, The University of Southern California, among others.

Monica also believes very strongly in giving back to the community and puts her heart, hands and wallet to work by contributing to the **Giveback Homes** mission to build homes for families in need throughout the US and Central America

You can connect with her at MonicaRivera.com or via email at Monica@MonicaRivera.com.

A LOVE NOTE FROM MONICA

Hey there, I'm so glad you're here! Thank you for sharing in my story. As a token of my appreciation, I'd like to offer you a gift, *de un corazon a otro*. From my heart to yours.

For a free audio recording of **The Chingona Manifesto**™ and to join my private community of like-minded hustlers y *chingonas poderosas* please visit: TheChingonaManifesto.com

THE CLASSY CHINGONA'S GUIDE TO SETTING YOURSELF UP FOR SUCCESS

"And while she never felt quite normal, she was nowhere near crazy. She just loved too much. Choosing to see the savage world through her heart instead of her eyes."

—Jessica Michelle, poet and artist

Growing up in Los Angeles, California, you are exposed to the smoke and mirrors of Hollywood at a young age. You are also exposed to a variety of cultures and traditions that are different from your own. At the same time, you learn to be proud of your heritage.

Which is why growing up speaking Spanish and English simultaneously was something that I not only loved, but also found to be completely natural.

I always viewed my rich Latino heritage as an asset, not a liability. However, as I would come to find out in elementary school, even though I thought of myself as a Latina, that wasn't the case outside my casita (home).

In all actuality, I was teased for not being "Latina enough" and called a sellout for getting good grades and wanting to go to college. I was repeatedly called a "coconut" for being "brown on the outside but white on the inside." Many called me ungrateful for not realizing how "lucky"

I had it, because I could "pass" as Caucasian. I'm still not sure what was worse, being told I didn't look or act Latina enough or the assumption I would want to "pass" for anything other than who I was. Frankly, I still don't understand how this is even a claim people make.

It's safe to say, I learned at a young age that being a Latina woman in the United States, was seen by many as something to hide, not embrace. I was labeled a "double negative" for not only being a minority, but also a woman.

However, I had a secret power that combatted everything "they" said to me. A secret power that empowered me to take on whatever life had to throw at me or what others said and confidently respond with a smile.

You see, my mother and abuelita raised me to be a *Classy Chingona*™!!

Yup, you read that right.

A **Classy Chingona**™, or "CC" for short, is a woman who knows what she wants and isn't afraid to speak up for it. She's a born leader, proudly bicultural and a woman who stands in her own power without apology. And while she isn't afraid to work hard, she's also wise enough to figure out how to work smarter. Why? So she can spend more time with those she loves, doing the things she loves. And while she's always classy, if the situation calls for it, she doesn't shy away from being sassy. You see, she's a true guerrera (warrior) who can hold her own and also boldly stands up for those who can't stand up for themselves. She also recognizes that if she doesn't set her boundaries, others will do it for her. When others see her, it's clear she means business and has no time for nonsense. Those who mistake her kindness for weakness, quickly learn she is anything but weak. A *Classy Chingona*™ is on a mission to change the world, a day at a time, using her own unique gifts to turn her dreams into reality, to be of service, and leave a legacy.

Without a doubt, my mom and abuelita (grandmother) shaped me to be the passionate *Classy Chingona*™ I am today.

We came up with the term, *Classy Chingona*™ when I was in elementary school. However, it took on a deeper meaning the day I was leaving for college and my mom dropped me off at the airport.

Even though I couldn't be more excited to get to the East Coast, the reality of what I was leaving behind to do so, hit me all at once that afternoon.

As the first person to go to college in my family, I missed the memo letting me know it's totally normal for parents to go with their children to college and help them move in. As a matter of fact, it's totally weird if they don't. As they say, hindsight really is 20/20.

But not knowing any better, I gave in to my teenage ego, which told me I was a big girl and had it all under control. And so, I had asked my mom, months earlier, not to come with me. And get this, she listened! Of all times to listen to me, she chose this moment. Ay Dios mio. LOL.

It wasn't until we reached the airport that morning that I realized the mistake I had made.

"Wait, what do you mean I'm not going to see you until Parent's Weekend? That's eight weeks away," I frantically asked her, as she kissed me goodbye.

In that moment, it hit me like a ton of bricks. I wasn't ready to face college by myself. So, I immediately asked her to come with me.

"Lizza, remember this is what you wanted. I asked you repeatedly if you were sure, because I wouldn't be able to buy a last minute ticket for a flight," she calmly answered with a slight crack in her voice.

As she tells me now, it was as much of a growing pain for her as it was for me. Letting me go 3,000 miles away from home, even if it was for school, was no easy task for her or my abuelita. However, she was confident that this would be the first of many lessons I needed to learn…on my own. So she held strong.

Just staring at her, I could tell she wanted to cry just as much as I did. But in true *Classy Chingona*™ style, she didn't. Instead, she looked at me and said, "But mija (daughter) you won't be alone. Your abuelita and I will be there with you every step of the way, inside you.

You see, we've been raising you to be an independent, yet compassionate woman since the day you were born. We did everything we could to encourage you to step into your light and shine, and still have a loving heart.

- When you get lonely, reach out.
- When you see someone in need of a friend, introduce yourself.
- When you see someone being mean to someone else, step in.
- When you need to call us, day or night, pick up the phone.
- When you encounter a "no," look for another way to "yes."
- When your abilities are doubted, focus on your work and let it speak for itself.
- When you feel like giving up, remember you are standing on our shoulders. And if we aren't throwing in the towel, you definitely aren't either.

Lizza, it's now your turn to take the baton and run this leg of the race the next four years. This is where you get to show the world the *Classy Chingona*™

we raised you to be and lead by example for those coming after you!"

As I watched my mom nervously get into her car, images of the three of us over the years flashed before me. And even though I would have done anything to have her get on that plane with me, I fully understood what she met. Whether I liked it or not, the "baton" had been passed and it was up to me to step up and into my new role. I came of age on that day, as part of my youth died, and a part of my womanhood blossomed in its place.

Just like my mother and abuelita had been fierce leaders in my life, it was time for me to be one as well.

And just like that the **Classy Chingonas Circle™** was born and my mom, abuelita and I were the founding members. We were multi-generational and multi-cultural Latinas, united by our passion for our family, dreams, and justice, and fueled by our love of one another.

You see after my parents divorced, my mother and abuelita raised me and gave me the best gift a child could ever receive: unconditional love.

They also gave me the best of old traditions mixed with modern day feminism.

My abuelita used to say, "una gente esta tan pobre que no mas tienen dinero." Which translates to, "some people are so poor, all they have is money." Meaning that by just focusing on making money, happiness and love will always evade you. But, if instead you focus on sharing love and living in your purpose, the money will be there. She also raised me to know that my actions would speak ten times louder than my words ever could.

My mom, on the other hand, taught me that success and money were mine for the taking, regardless of my gender, or my financial or ethnic background. Her work ethic and drive showed me what was possible when you show up at 100% every day ready to work on your dreams. Despite never going to a traditional college, getting married and divorced at a young age, raising a child and taking care of her mother simultaneously, my mother is a successful entrepreneur. She has made a name for herself in the hair industry as a celebrity hair colorist and as the owner of an upscale hair salon in Orange County, California.

And whilst she didn't attend a traditional college, my mom is one of the most educated women I know. She is constantly taking new classes and graduating from programs both in and out of her field. So it is no surprise she is a leader in her industry. She has taught hands-on classes on the most elite stages in the hair industry around the world. I've never seen anyone more talented with a hair color wand than her. Her hair-coloring work is flawless. And her constant drive for self development is infectious. I totally inherited my thirst for knowledge from her. She has molded life into a living classroom and taught me to do the same.

My abuelita taught us both that education, the love in our hearts and experiences were the three things no one would ever be able to take from us. These are the true priceless riches we can all have. It's our personal choice how much of each is possible. And thanks to the internet, the possibilities of what we can learn and do are endless.

It is also not surprising then, that many of our mother-daughter "playdates" often involved going to the book store or library to pick out the latest releases that called to us. We would spend countless hours in there, though it would only ever feel like minutes. Since I was only allowed to have educational toys growing up, books were everything to me. They allowed me to not only travel to far off places, but, also to learn, experiment, and explore my curiosities.

These two *Classy Chingonas*™ taught me first hand that it isn't where we start that matters, but where we finish. Based on their teachings, I've accomplished quite a bit in my life and devised the *Classy Chingona*™ Success System to help others set themselves up for success as well. And while I did luck out getting raised by these two remarkable women, it's probably the only time you'll see me use the word "luck."

As a modern-day, renaissance woman, who's made a name for herself acting on stage and the big screen, hosting TV shows in English and Spanish, and creating content for brands and my online community, I'm often told how "lucky" I am.

- "Lucky" to have a successful career.

- "Lucky" to have my own company.

- "Lucky" to have financial freedom.

- "Lucky" to have been the first in my family to attend and graduate from college.

- "Lucky" to have an Ivy League education.

- "Lucky" to have a life that I love.

- And, as I mentioned earlier, "lucky" to be able to "pass" for Caucasian. (Again, how is this even a thing, right?)

The "lucky" list goes on and on, but I think you get the point. As a matter of fact, I'm willing to bet you have been called "lucky" once or twice in your life too.

Here's the thing about these statements, they're hurtful and dismissive to the hard work we've put into each personal and professional goal.

While I understand that when people talk about someone being "lucky," they don't necessarily mean to insult him or her, but that's what they are doing. If you look up the definition of "lucky" or "luck" you'll get some variation of this:

"Good fortune; advantage or success, considered as the result of chance, rather than one's own actions."

Think about that for a second. When we call someone "lucky" for the greatness showing up in their life, we're essentially dismissing all the hard work they have put in daily. Whether it's getting a job promotion, losing weight or even buying a new car, we wipe away all their efforts when we call them "lucky."

It's as if we're telling the person they don't deserve the opportunity, happiness, or success that is showing up in their life, because they didn't earn it. That all the sacrifices, discipline, and consistent action they did was all for nothing. My inner *Classy Chingona*™ is already rolling her eyes and thinking, *"Excuse me, but no."* Is that you too?

As the saying goes, "Words have power, choose them carefully." And under the current framework, the word "lucky" makes me feel like anything, but a "lucky duck."

As you start setting up your *Classy Chingona* ™ Success System, I invite you to not only be careful about the words you use, but also be careful with those you accept as truth in your life.

Why is this "lucky" talk important? What does this have to do with leadership?

Well, after traveling more than 300,000 miles around this beautiful planet of ours, I've seen first-hand just how badly people want to be "lucky." Whether it's lucky in love, business, wealth, health, or just plain happy-go-lucky (aka really happy). It doesn't matter where on the planet you're from, this desire to get what we want out of life is a core desire.

However, there are some key differences between those who do get "lucky" and those who don't.

Now, I'm sure you are wondering how I can believe in creating our own "luck" after just breaking down why I find it insulting.

Here's the thing about luck: the harder you work, the "luckier" you get.

> *"Luck is what happens when preparation meets opportunity."*
> —Seneca, Roman philosopher

This quote has been a guiding principle for me since I was a child. The truth it packs sits at the foundation of my success toolbox. The same toolbox this chapter will unpack for you.

My vision is to empower you to create the life you dream of, but might not know how to create.

If I can show you how to follow the path to creating what you want right now, would you take it?

Yes, or *hell* yes?

If I set you on the path to receiving more opportunity, joy, and success in your life, would you be ready to jump in?

Si or *claro que* si?

If you're still here reading, stop for five seconds, and give yourself a pat on the back, RIGHT NOW!

Go ahead. I'll wait. Seriously, do it now. (You'll understand why in a moment.)

5, 4, 3, 2, 1 . . .

Andddd, we're back. Woot! Woot!

You see, when you answered "yes" to these two questions, your mindset already started to shift. You made a conscious soul contract with yourself and set the intention to be, do, and have more in your life.

As American filmmaker Woody Allen has said, "80% of success is just showing up."

And here you are. Showing up, ready to thrive, not just survive this thing called life. So go ahead and give yourself that pat on the back now, if you didn't do it the first time. After you're done, go ahead and make yourself a cup of tea or un cafecito (coffee) and get ready to work.

TOOLS NEEDED

1. Your favorite pen(s) and highlighter(s)

2. Journal, notebook, or printed worksheet

3. Your personal calendar or favorite calendar app

4. An open mind

5. Visit www.xoxolizza.com/classychingonabonus and download and print your complementary bonuses.

6. A candle

LET'S BEGIN...

If you look up the habits of successful people, you will find that a daily morning ritual is a common trait among them. What you choose to do during your morning ritual will vary, depending on what you are working on, your time constraints or simply your state of mind. Rest assured, there is no one right way. However, I will tell you that consistently taking action and doing your morning ritual every day for 40 days straight, even if only for 5 minutes, will change your life.

Here is the *Classy Chingona*™ guide to setting yourself up for success.

1. Light your candle, close your eyes, and take three deep breaths.

2. On your exhale, focus on the word "calm."

3. Place your hand over your heart and speak with passion as you say these words:

    "I easily let go of the thoughts that hold me back, and I embrace the infinite potential available to me in the Universe today."
    (Repeat six times)

4. Using your journal or the downloadable "Brain Dump Worksheet," write the date at the top of the page and do a brain dump. Literally, list every single thing that pops up in your head that you have to do today. By getting it out of your head and onto paper, you are able to give your ideas and plans a place to rest, and can designate the time they will demand of you. You'll also easily identify what items matter in the immediate future, down the line, and what can be delegated or simply removed from the list.

5. Once you're done, reread your brain dump list and circle **THREE** actions that **NEED** to be done **TODAY**. Three action items, big or small, that will make you feel successful by getting them over and done with today. Trust me, I know you have more than three items listed. That's not to say you won't get to those as well. For now, however, I want you to focus on the three actions that help move you forward in any way. *Note: this can be as simple as making a scary

phone call to someone about collaborating.

6. Once you've identified your three success actions, write them at the top of your journal or your downloadable "Success Action Worksheet." Choose to write the one you want to do the least at the top of your list. More on this in Step 8. These three actions are the basis of your daily "success action list." Your success action list differs from a typical to-do list in that it clearly identifies what's important for the day. A standard to-do list doesn't distinguish between urgent, important and simple errands. And most people default to working on their to-do list in the order they happen to write it in (aka their brain dump list).

7. While the *Classy Chingona*™ Success System is all about taking action, the secret sauce is in making sure we are taking inspired action. Anyone can be busy, but we are looking to make you laser focused, so more opportunities show up. And what happens when opportunity and preparation meet? You get "lucky!" (wink, wink. LOL.) This is also how you work smarter, not harder. The more you are aligned with your long term vision, the easier it becomes to identify the next step in your master plan. One way I keep my master plan moving forward is to identify what daily "ship" I can send out into the Universe.

> *"A ship in harbor is safe but that is not what ships are built for."*
>
> —John A. Shedd, US author, professor

Much like the quote above states, a ship's job is to be sent out in search of treasure. So, what one action can you take TODAY that allows you to reach for a goal outside your comfort zone? Is there perhaps a person you met at a conference you can contact to set up a meeting? Is there an influencer who your brand, or you as an individual, wants to collaborate with? If so, look up their contact information on social media and send them your bio and a pitch of your idea. The goal here isn't to just get a "yes" to every pitch, which would be amazing if you did, but to also make sure you are sending out at least 30 "ships" every month. The more that go out, the higher the chance that at least one will return with that proverbial treasure. If you do this long enough, it becomes a regular occurrence for ships to return daily with "treasure" of some sort.

8. The next step is to identify and eat your "frog" of the day. The key here is to "eat" it, aka get it done, first thing in the morning. The idea comes from US author Mark Twain's quote that said, "Eat a live frog first thing in the morning and nothing worse will happen to you the rest of the day." So, when looking at your daily "success action list," which you created in Step 6, what is the largest, most important task you need to do today? You know, the one you will most likely want to procrastinate, if you don't take immediate action? Highlight it and plan on doing that first, after you finish setting up your day.

9. This is one of my favorite steps. The longer you follow the *Classy Chingona*™ Success System, the more you will find "lucky" coincidences happen in your life. You find the perfect parking spot, you bump into an old friend you have been thinking of lately, or you might even find money you forgot you put away for safe keeping. So, to keep track of all this "luck" you are creating, you will write three things you are grateful for today on the bottom of your "Success Action Worksheet" or in your journal. These can be big or small occurrences in your life. You will find the more grateful you are for the good showing up in your life, the more you will find to be grateful for. It's a wonderful paradoxical catch-22 situation.

10. Here comes the fun part. Now that you have set up your day for success on paper, your next step is to schedule your three items on your calendar. Take out your calendar or open your preferred

calendar app and schedule the time you will make that phone call, work on your report, write for an hour uninterrupted, or simply mark the time you need to leave your office to get to your next meeting a few minutes early. Scheduling what needs to get done is another common trait highly successful people share. Everyone from Sir Richard Branson and Oprah to Olympic gold medalists and New York Times bestselling authors that I've interviewed over the years, all agree that if it's not in your calendar, it won't get done. Of course, always leave room for unpredicted blessings to show up in your day.

11. EXECUTE!! That's right. You plan your work, so you can then work your plan. You've identified what inspired actions you need to take and have made room for them in your day. All that's left is for you to take action.

12. Studies show you have a higher rate of completing a project if you take immediate action, big or small, within the first five seconds of getting the idea to start. Which is why re-reading your list throughout the day is key. For this step, take a picture of your success action list so it's in your phone. Then set at least three alarms on your phone. When the alarm sounds, take a minute to look over your success action list. As in, actually read it word for word, don't just quickly glance at it. As you read, do a mental review. What have you already accomplished and checked off? What items do you have left? If you are done with all of them, what items can you move over from your brain dump list? You'll move through your list faster this way and will feel a sense of accomplishment each time you see how much you have already completed.

There you have it. Your *Classy Chingona*™ guide to setting yourself up for success. By strategically planning your day and shifting your mindset to expect the best out of the day, you are now ready for whatever the Universe has in store for you.

As my high school tennis coach once told me, "If you stay ready, you'll never lose time getting ready." This lesson applies to life on and off the court.

I'd love to keep in touch and hear about your own *Classy Chingona*™ journey to outrageous happiness and success fulfillment. Make sure you visit www.xoxolizza.com/classychingonabonus to join my worldwide circle of *Classy Chingonas*™!! This is my exclusive reader's site, where you'll be able to download some sweet bonuses to keep you on track and organized.

EEK! I can hardly wait for you to see, and most importantly experience, how the Classy Chingona™ Success System can change your life. And this is just the beginning, as I have so much more in store for my fellow "CC's" this year. This includes the release of my own book, which not only dives deeper into the Classy Chingona™ Success System, but is an overall success manual for the modern-day power Latina. Of course, all my fellow "CC's" who click the link above will get early access to ordering the book, live workshop tickets and a bunch of useful bonuses. Stay tuned!!

If we haven't already connected on all things social, I invite you to add **@xoxolizza** on your favorite social media app. Once you do, I invite you to say "hi" and use our **#ClassyChingonas** hashtag so I know you are in our posse.

You will find me posting my daily adventures around the world, as well as my favorite finds, tips and even giveaways on *Periscope, Snapchat, Instagram, Twitter* and *YouTube*. I also enjoy livesteaming on www.Facebook.com/lizzamonetmorales.

I look forward to hearing from you and learning more about your personal journey.

Until then, keep shining like the *Classy Chingona*™ you were born to be.

xoxo,

Lizza

LIZZA MONET MORALES

Lizza Monet Morales, aka @xoxolizza, is an actor, tv host and content creator in both English and Spanish. She has leveraged her love of tech, fashion, and inspirational messages to create a global social media fanbase (LoveBug Nation) while becoming one of the top Latinas in entertainment media. In 2016, she won the TECLA Award for *Best Live Creator*, which was the first award ever  given to a live streamer by any award show. And in 2017 she won TECLA's *Best Live Creator* award for the second year in a row. She was named one of the "20 Most Influential Latinos and Latinas of 2016" by *Alegeria* magazine and was nominated for the 2017 Shorty Award as *Periscoper Of The Year*.

On Women's Day 2016, *Periscope* featured Lizza on the app as one of their 13 "#sheinspires" women from around the world. After travelling close to 300,000 miles around the globe in 2015, she's was dubbed the "Carmen San Diego of Livestream." She continues to be the highest ranked Latina on *Periscope*, garnering close to 8 million hearts, aka likes, for her broadcasts. When not on *Periscope*, you can catch her on *Facebook Live, Snapchat, Instagram Stories, Twitter, Patreon* and *YouTube*.

In the spring of 2016, Ms. Morales was invited by FLOTUS Michelle Obama to attend *The United States Of Women Summit* as one of the country's "agents of change." In the fall of 2016, she was invited by President Barrack Obama to attend his *South By South Lawn* (SXSL) conference at The White House. During the 2016 election cycle, she served as a judge for *VotoLatino* and FUSE Media's *Crash The Parties* competition, alongside *Emmy* award-winning host Rachel Maddow and NPR's Maria Hinojosa.

On the fashion front, IMG, which produces the most impactful Fashion Week events around the globe, named Lizza one of their global committee experts for their DHL Exported fashion designer competition for 2015-2016. She was one of six experts picked, which included acclaimed designer Nicole Miller and *Vogue Italy*'s Sara Maino.

Lizza has been on-air for *Access Hollywood*, Telemundo, *EXTRA*, Univision, *Celebrity Justice*, *The Insider* and The TV-Guide Channel among others. In addition, she has reported for *Us Weekly*, *People Magazine* and was a featured columnist in *Item Magazine*.

As an actor, she was most recently seen in David Mamet's *Phil Spector* biopic for HBO starring Al Pacino and Helen Mirren. She was also a series regular on VH1's *New York Goes To Hollywood*.

As a bilingual digital influencer, Lizza has worked with a variety of Fortune 500, 100 and 50 brands to create and implement engaging campaigns and activations for product launches, film openings, tv premieres, reviews and more. These include, but are not limited to Microsoft, Nike, Ford, Red Bull, Sears, AT&T and CoverGirl. She also works as a consultant and strategist for companies big and small.

She's been featured on *The Conan O'Brien Show*, CNN and NPR and in *AdWeek*, *Cosmo for Latinas* and *Latina*.

Lizza attended Harvard University and Middlebury College, where she graduated with a bachelor's degree in Political Science and double minor in Economics and Japanese. She also earned a post-graduate journalism certificate from UCLA and is a graduate of the Atlantic Theater Company's master conservatory program.

Make sure to also visit www.xoxolizza.com/classychingonabonus to claim your bonus material and join our global **Classy Chingonas Circle**™. Also, make sure to follow **@xoxolizza** on your favorite social media app and say "hello." She'll love hearing from you.

SOMETIMES STANDING UP

MEANS WALKING AWAY

The greatest story in my life is the one about my children and me. I'm the proud mama of two beautiful, intelligent, loving daughters. They are the reason for my existence. When they were each born I fell in love with my babies, and my love for them has just continued to grow, along with my admiration. If anything in this life keeps me close to the Lord it's my children and the need I have for God to protect them and bless them. The work I do and the journey I've lived, they've lived with me. I always think of the Gilmore Girls as an example of a woman (me) who had a tumultuous relationship with her mother, who grew up to have a blast raising her wonderful daughters in pure love. I was a young mom with 2 daughters by 24, and twice single by 30. I needed a Christian marriage and when that wasn't what was offered, I separated and raised my girls myself. The key to our relationship has been support, trust, and God's love and he's blessed me richly because I'm so proud of everything they are and do. I love talking to them and sharing their life, and nothing could ever change the appreciation I feel for each one. Throughout my adult life there's never been a moment when anyone or anything could ever come close to being as important. I know how much God loves me because they are in my life.

I have not accomplished everything I dream of, and I have not yet obtained all the desires of my heart, but I am satisfied when I realize that in every step and phase of this journey, I have been learning and experiencing a great life. Mine is a life where I know I'm blessed every day, and I'm supported by the people I love. My relationships are meaningful, and I cherish them more than ever now that with added maturity, I can fully appreciate their worth. Love is the answer for me. Love is one of the BIG words in my life, along with a whole bunch of other meaningful words, like sorrow, forgiveness, commitment, promise, fairness, justice, and truth.

Trying to build a business or a professional career in today's work environment can be challenging and many times frustrating if you find yourself like I do, desperate for change or a new challenge. I have to keep learning and moving forward; it's a thing with me. I've accepted this and a whole lot of other quirks as just part of my DNA. I'm simply blessed with many *BIG IDEAS* and *DREAMS* that I insist on living out. I'm convinced these *DREAMS* and *BIG IDEAS* were seeded in my heart long before I was born, making my path prophetic because no matter what gets in my way, eventually and lovingly, Jesus is making a way for me just as He promised when He gave me my name. I work hard in lining up my professional life, while keeping straight my alignment with God. Because success is never a straight line forward or upward, I'm not worried so much. Even when I'm busy constantly pushing through a long list of distractions and setbacks that show up to be dealt with. My life is bag of mixed nuts and I've learned to be well with it all.

Business is a challenge for me. Like a rollercoaster, it offers great heights and the fear of steep financial falls, but even with all the uncertainty, it's still exhilarating and fun. Entrepreneurship offers me the opportunity to bring vision and solutions to fill an existing gap in the market place. In my case, the gap lies in the much needed bilingual content and services that I continually develop to assure our immigrant workforce can be provided increased access to training and development opportunities.

Professionally I'm a bilingual workforce development professional, dedicated to creating adult learning and professional training opportunities in Spanish for the Latino labor market in the US and abroad. I do this by creating innovative delivery options and content to up-skill our local workforce.

I have a lot of competition but I've realized over time that it's not coming from anyone who is just like me, having walked my life's journey to have my perspective, heart, vision, or my passion to see it through. I feel purposeful as I serve a population that are being passed up for investment in development opportunities going instead to others who are easier to serve, having less complicated barriers to employment and integration and who are less political to serve in times where immigration and jobs are such hot topics. I serve a now priority population that needs personal and professional development desperately. The status quo cannot continue without great consequences to our Latino workforce. The struggle continues to assure we don't leave struggling families behind as the labor market changes, and displaces our people through technological advances and other business trends they're not prepared for.

Conscious awareness as described by Jeff Klein in his series on "It's Just Good Business" is "a process of recognizing what is going on inside and outside, the effects of decisions and actions, the interaction between a complex array of factors and forces, fostering an expanded perspective, and openness to new possibilities." I love this description, because it explains my life perfectly, both personal and professional. Conscientious leadership is an excellent topic to consider and I'll help you to do so by sharing stories from my professional life that will illustrate the absence of mindful leadership and the many ways in which people can be affected. I'll share how I dealt with real life situations, and the patterns that I learned to recognize along the way.

I personally value authenticity and integrity in those I keep as friends, and those I partner with in business. People who are not authentic will waste your time and take you down an unreliable path; one that you cannot build on. I know this because I've honestly lost a lot of time going after opportunities that didn't pan out and what these situations all had in common was that *people* I dealt with either did not deliver what they promised, or I found out they were involved in shady business dealings and I had to walk away, leaving a quite a lot of money on the table. Money I worked hard for, and that my family needed. But I assessed and concluded that if it was money off the backs of others who were either scammed or abused, I didn't need it. I've learned that every situation we find ourselves in will lead us to important decisions that will show us who you are in each challenging moment. I'm not at all cynical, and on the contrary, I see opportunity everywhere but it's worth considering and being vigilant, by accessing periodically and with caution who we allow into our inner circle.

Some years ago my partner and I decided that as bilingual educators and serial entrepreneurs, we should get involved in real estate; mortgages to be specific. We had previously taught English as a second language and financial literacy. We believed that homeownership and financial education would help clients make better and more informed decisions when they ventured to buy a home. We believed we could make a difference for the many families we would serve. We knew homeownership to be a good thing for Latino families, where they could build wealth and equity which could transform their financial future and that of their children, and we wanted to help facilitate this process. So we learned the process, found a broker, and got our licenses within weeks, and "Las Maestras Mortgage" was born.

We did well in a very short time but we felt protective of our clients during our learning curve, so we insisted on learning by reviewing each case with loan officers before escrow. We learned as we worked by processing the files we brought in. The business proved to be quite lucrative, but over the coming months we began to see some troubling trends. We began to question things we sensed may be predatory practices. Every time we asked questions we were given vague answers, and we began to suspect that there may have been a reason we weren't getting clear answers to our questions. We were treated as if we asked *too* many questions! Does any of this feel familiar to any of you? Well, this only served to make us more determined to learn the truth and we weren't shy about asking.

Our questions became very specific, and we soon realized we were stepping on toes, asking about issues that were sensitive to the broker's fees and profits. The scandals about bad loans hadn't broken out on the news yet, so people were not forewarned about the predatory practices already happening, and they simply thought they were getting a great deal and the chance of a lifetime. Anyone with a level head could have realized how inflated everything was becoming but with easy financing terms, and the low level of documentation required to qualify for loans, the opportunity at hand was just too hard to pass up for people who had dreamed of having a home for so long. My partner and I noticed the rush to homeownership that was taking place especially in Southern California, and we witnessed how our Latino families had jumped at the chance to qualify and move into their dream homes. We watched as they made huge sacrifices to make it happen, and eventually many made promises to pay way beyond their means. Because we knew the consequences of these decisions we worried for them and tried to educate them on the details and terms before signing. In contrast, other industry professionals ignored their ethical responsibilities to their clients, instead losing their minds with the thought of making high profits fast.

Several things were beginning to trouble us. We all began to see prices start rising fast and bidding wars were breaking out and upping the ante for every loan. Once in love with the home, customers were caught up in a bidding war willing to pay far beyond the asking price in order to be the winning bidder. Winning came at a steep price for those who ran on emotion. My partner and I questioned the ethics and fiduciary responsibility of brokers, loan officers, and real estate agents. We felt that brokers and loan officers should not have raised the loan approval limits beyond what our customer's income would bare, but they made more money by doing it. We found out that our broker was placing our clients in loans that were harder or costlier to get out of, forcing them to pay high penalties if they refinanced. Of course, we found they made more money that way as well. We witnessed real estate agents showing our clients homes that had a ticket price much higher than what they were qualified to spend on a home, but of course they made more money when they sold a home with a higher loan amount. Soon after, rumors began to surface. You heard murmuring in the industry and on the news, that brokers and loan officers were providing low income customers with shady loans without fully explaining the terms. Our financial literacy classes began to fill with families who were now seeking help in understanding their loans in hopes of undoing the damage. Before they could get out from under the debt they had recently signed up for, the bubble burst and everything was turned upside down. Then came the crash. While families lost their homes, brokers, loan officers, and real estate agents walked off into the sunset without a worry, probably having a record year, never looking back. I imagine they justified it all as "just business".

I don't regret having been a part of that industry because I learned so much and it changed me. I learned to assess people as I meet them, by doing a mental value's check when meeting new potential partners. I learned that a lot of decisions are made in back rooms with closed doors, and unless you work inside a particular industry, you won't know how it really operates, what to watch out for, and who can get hurt when conflicts of interest are involved.

As a result of the experiences I've lived, I learn to trust my instincts and recognize the patterns in others so I can be forewarned and take precautions. Over time I've become more life and business savvy; direct about what concerns me. I also don't mind if I'm shown the door if you feel I'm asking too many questions or if I need certain assurances or concessions when working with others. I challenge myself to also bring my true self to the table so those who want a competent and caring partner will be able gauge where and what I stand for, and feel comfortable working with me.

When you are fortunate to find wonderful people to work with it's great because you're free to share openly and you know you can get some support. My best friend and business partner has known me over 30 years, since our children were young. Our relationship is built on our history together, which includes many beautiful memories and the trust that has been built over good times and bad. It's gold! Working with people who are passionate about the same things, who can share their struggles and their life's moments with you is priceless. I've learned that relationships are important, and the kind of relationships I can build will depend on my trustworthiness and performance, and the fair dealing and integrity of the people I'm working with.

All day long in doing business, I plan on joining with, and finding the people I need to connect with to move my plans forward, but the success of my efforts, I know, will depend directly on the conscientiousness and reliability of everyone involved. Part of the fair dealing we all need has to do with others in positions of power simply being gracious and opening the door for those on the outside knocking. I've seen both sides and this gives me a huge advantage when I evaluate how I'm being treated. I've met wonderful people who saw value in my work and my heart and they have invited me in and have given me a seat at the table. They encouraged me to bring my Latina flavor and my perspective to the group and gave me a platform to advocate for my people. How wonderful these moments have been. I don't think they knew how much this would mean to me, but I made sure to tell them of my gratitude and appreciation. It has been the start of wonderful friendships that have been cultivated over time.

My true calling and expertise is in workforce development. My career path began early but right on time. Just before my 15 th birthday we moved from East LA where I was born to immigrant parents from Mexico. As a single mom, she worried for our safety and moved mountains to buy a home in OC, affording it only by breaking her back cleaning 5-7 houses a day to make the mortgage. That first summer in a new safer neighborhood, I applied for a summer youth job. These were jobs developed to provide disadvantaged youth with opportunity by facilitating employment and work experience. I always believed that God had a path for me because I was placed to work that summer in the State of California Employment Development Department office, which served job seekers with employment services and unemployment insurance if they lost their job.

I was trained to be of service to the public, to assess their experience and technical skills, and match them up with new jobs, faxed in daily from local employers. I loved it! Constantly learning and growing and helping others. I worked with wonderful career professionals who taught the ropes and provided me with excellent examples of leadership. They mentored me, put up with me, and used me, putting to good use my skills as a bilingual youth to translate for Spanish speakers during UI (unemployment insurance) interviews. It was there I began to believe that I can make a difference where ever God placed me. I realized my sensitivity to the plight of immigrants, who reminded me of my family, and I experience the power of bilingualism and bilingual pay. Throughout my career I have repeatedly said, "Yes, you can pay me more because I'm bilingual." Yes, of course you can! LOL!

Being bilingual, bicultural and impassioned to serve in Spanish, I had long since concluded that being born in the USA was not only a huge blessing, but also an enormous responsibility. I grew up around my Tias (aunts) who each emigrated from Mexico when I was young. They went to college and became professionals in industry, and business owners. Being part of an immigrant family, I witnessed first how my family worked hard and strived to get ahead. My mom now had a housekeeping business, and my step father was a small manufacturer of custom wrought iron fences. I saw the struggle and the confusion my family went through, including long feverish nights brought on my so much worry, and the pressure to meet arbitrary deadlines set by random inspectors, because so much was falling through the cracks. These external and internal problems brought on so much uncertainly, and as children we felt it, and were affected by it. The language and cultural barriers caused many issues, and clarifying any of them required an interpreter. I was my family's 14 year old interpreter for all notices, contracts, mortgage docs and bank statements.

Some years ago, I was working with a colleague, under contract for a community college in our district. The director who hired us also oversaw the Small Business Development Center sponsored by the SBA. We developed an entrepreneurial training program curriculum, wrote a proposal on their behalf, and it got it funded. The program was a big success bringing new funds to deliver basic business training to emerging entrepreneurs. As we began to develop the curriculum with my colleagues for our entrepreneurial training program, of course I thought back to what I'd seen at home while growing up knowing this program would help Latino business owners if it was delivered in their first language. I requested a meeting with our director and asked if we could offer the program in Spanish? The answer was no, but I was given the opportunity to use a classroom if I could get an interested group together. I set out to prove the need. On the first day of our 10 week program I had nearly 40 students and the retention was impressive. My enrollment goal was 25.

The interest, attendance, and retention were there. In order to maintain the Spanish entrepreneurial program, I founded a non-profit and the Latin Business Institute was born in 1997. I learned that if one door wasn't open I could find another way, and if that didn't work, I could create a new door.

Have you ever been fired or lost a contract opportunity for doing the right thing? I have. I once worked for a major staffing agency in Irvine, CA. I was hired as an on-site HR staffer and my job was sourcing employees for a firm that packaged CD's into small book sized boxes. Maybe 30 to 50 CD's per box. Most of their existing employees were Spanish speakers therefore I concluded that clearly English was not necessary to the job. Once recruitment began I noticed many of the applicants that were applying had previously worked close by as seasonal migrant workers picking strawberries. Hard back-breaking work. I felt wonderful being in a position to offer them more stable work with better pay.

Many of these applicants asked me to help them fill out their application and as I had always done before I offered my help filling out their applications. I knew the law. English only rules can only apply if the work requires it, and since the majority of existing workers spoke only Spanish I knew there wouldn't be a problem. But I was wrong. Turned out I was being watched by a Latino colleague seeking points with the owner for his own job security. He complained that I was speaking Spanish and helping Spanish speakers with their applications. I knew there was no integrity in ignoring a need for help when I was capable of assisting. I knew these job applicants qualified to do the work. I took hold of my personal truth, which is that no one can ever pay me enough to speak only English directly to someone I know cannot understand me. I was warned, and when I chose to continue speaking Spanish as needed, I was fired. And so my fate was sealed!

To this day I wear that firing as a badge of honor. It is my honor to serve my community in any way I can. My faith tells me that I'll always be covered when I do the right thing. I learned that working for firms who don't care about people is not a good match for me. I can't stand injustice and I can't be part of it, no matter the cost. I consider it shameful that it was a Latino male who intentionally affected my livelihood, and that of my family, and who knows how many others. Sadly, it would not be the only time a successful Latino tried to impede me from helping others gain better employment opportunities.

I once approached an industrial bakery to offer training and development services. I had several meetings with the plant manager, who after speaking with me and viewing the curriculum, told me how great it was and how much he believed in training. He share with me that training similar to this had been offered years ago, and that 5 employees including him had benefited immensely. In fact he said that he was now the plant manager and the others were supervisors as a direct result. We worked out the funding to cover the cost so it was a win-win-win. At our next meeting he sat me down and asked me to look at the computer monitors on his desk, which were actually live cameras of the workers on the production floor. He told me that those employees I was watching on the monitor were happy because they knew their job. He said "They are filling the box with cookies and placing the label, filling the box and placing the label. Simple!" He told me that if I came in and provided them training and education, I would be lighting them up with new possibilities. Then they wouldn't be happy filling the box and placing the label. They would want more. He abruptly cancelled all plans for training. It was so shady for him to know that he had benefited so much from a training opportunity, but choose to turn around and shut the door on those seeking advancement beneath him. Surprisingly, less than a year after this occurred, the plant was shut down. Too many costly mistakes that could have been avoided through training. He lost his job as well, and from what I was later told, he and his family suffered from his long term unemployment. I'm glad to know he's landed safely in a new job now, but what about all the others?

In 2010 I worked for an awesome company; a high tech giant with 70 plants worldwide. I became their Training and Development Manager in an environment that provided everything you needed to create, develop, implement, and stretch your vision of what was possible in a career. It was an R&D plant, in which I worked with everyone on all levels, from the CEO & HR, engineers to production; everyone knew each other and worked across the board as a great team. No one cared what you wore, the dress code was casual, and time in and out was flexible, because they only cared about the work, the morale, and the results. It was heaven with a hefty salary and a great benefit package. Then 9/11 happened. I remember management knew this was a moment in time that would change everything and they set up several TVs in the lunchroom and we were invited to spend any amount of time throughout the day watching the news coverage. I remember feeling that this was a different kind of company. A special company that had great vision and one that cared about their people. Unfortunately, Tele-communications took a dive on the stock market and the plant was unfortunately closed down. We received a generous severance package, which proved to us that this company was interested in taking care of their employees even as we were on our way out. Their brand stood for excellence in the workplace and they walked the walk.

A few months later I went to work as an Employee Resource Director for a firm that manufactured high end stainless steel kitchenware for hospitals, hotels and the 1%. I was immediately thrown into a state of shock as I experienced along with approximately 450 Latino production workers, the hell that can be a hostile workplace, the total opposite of conscientious leadership. This company knew every trick in the book to make a profit and squeeze their employees. They skimmed off employees checks, after having them work 6 or 7 (12 hour) days a week, they practiced nepotism, and favoritism for their own twisted purposes and methods to operate their plant. They discussed private performance issues with other employees, using some as snitches and spies to fabricate issues, in order to fire pre-selected people or harassed them. They knowingly used and misused undocumented workers and placed them in harm's way. They fired people unjustly. The stress was unbearable at times as I tried to do my job with integrity while witnessing this constant injustice. When the workers tried to organize they hired some big guns to spy on them, and intimidate them. They immediately fired anyone they found was involved in organizing or educating workers, and they willfully operated above the law because they felt safe to, always having attorneys on retainer to deal with the fall out.

I hadn't worked there more than 4 months when I knew I couldn't stay, but I thought of the workers who depended on having someone to talk to, who would advocate for them and support them in all the ways they were being affected because of the work environment and the nasty politics. As "Employee Relations" this fell squarely in my job description, and I was committed to stay longer. One morning there was a serious accident. We had a Safety Director who worked hand in hand with HR who was calling all the shots. Accidents were becoming more and more frequent and I sensed many incidents were being left unreported to authorities; in this case OSHA. This one was serious. A young man nearly lost his arm. I remember going out into the plant to check on the machine he had been using so I could document anything relevant which was part of my job dealing with employee issues. What I found was upsetting and immoral.

The young man was a sheet metal cutter using a huge machine that cut slabs of sheet metal. His arm somehow got stuck while the machine continued to operate, and he was seriously cut and rushed to the hospital. I found the safety button which should stop the machine in an emergency such as getting a piece of clothing, or worst a body part was caught up during the cutting process. The button was taped down and glued so that it would not function. There were 12 such machines on the floor. I decided to audit them all. I found and documented that all 12 had either gum, or glue or tape covering it so that it would not function. I honestly couldn't believe it how a company could place people's lives on the line for bigger profits. I was later told by a mechanic that the safety buttons were disabled so that production never stops. I knew the price. I took action anyways. I went back to my office, prayed and then I called OSHA to report the accident and my findings. Soon after they realized it was me who called it in I was fired. They said I was not a team player because I didn't just go along with everything. After all I was making a great salary. I found out repeatedly that I could not be bought. I knew the price for my decisions and I was fine with the consequences. I could smile and stand confident as they walked me to the door.

Conscientious leaders are those who can recognize there is a higher purpose in their life, family and work and that we're all inter connected. We serve to create trusting relationships and trust worthy organizations that can be counted on to be fair in everything, including hiring, promoting, contracting, and compensation amongst other employment benefits and terms. I always encourage others to seek out work with organizations that empower their people, allowing them to also grow to fulfil their purpose, because we all need that.

We cannot fool ourselves into thinking that a company or business person who has built a business on the backs of people they've taken advantage of will treat you any better. Good business leaders seek to be fair in all cases and empower their people to develop and become their best self. In my experience I've found bad leadership is not that hard to recognize because you'll find a pattern of conduct that reveals itself quickly. Nothing does more to demotivate workers than perceived unfairness such as nepotism or favoritism. Many of the workers I've trained have often told me that before I showed up, no one had offered them training in Spanish or any language. Most of these workers have spent 9 years, 17 years, 23 years, working for the same employer, with no development opportunities. This saddens me and makes me mad. Mad enough to want to change things. I know I do the work I do because many in the workforce don't have the support and knowledge they need to advance in the workplace, and they need change. I want a part in making this happen. It takes grit, guts, and great determination if you want to maintain your values and your principled way of dealing with others. Not everyone you come into contact with in work or business is principled. Many are very short sighted and selfish. They have little heart for others, and won't think twice about backstabbing you, stealing from you, or getting you fired simply for helping others, if it doesn't suit them. I've found a way forward by keeping God's order. My personal priorities are 1) Faith 2) Family 3) Community 4) Business, in that order. It is my belief that this is God's order for my life, and as much as I want to be successful, it cannot be at the cost of these priorities. I'm convinced that all due blessings will and do come in His perfect time, and that my family and I are covered when we sacrifice to serve Him, care for our family and build our community. Doors will open and I'd rather wait, while preparing for the wonderful gift and blessings of mind and heart that will surround me as I dedicate my life to my Lord who never leaves me, and always sustains me. One of my favorite verses is 2 Corinthians. It reads, "But he said to me, "My grace is sufficient for you, for My power is perfected in weakness." Therefore I will boast all the more gladly in my weakness, so that the power of Christ may rest upon me." This is the power that sustains, heals, and has restored my life many times.

In my personal life and family life there's been a series of challenges. One of the greater challenges has been caring for my mother who has heart problems and in March experienced another serious stroke. She's much weaker now and my daughters and I have been her primary caregivers for the past 10 years. I recently took more time to care for her, and as she becomes more frail, it's sometimes more difficult than I think I can handle. I have had to drop everything numerous times to be with her, making it very hard to focus. Through it all I come back to the desires of my heart, and I know that for as much as I want to seek my success I cannot fully engage in doing so, for now. We made a promise to my mother to keep her in her home no matter what happened, and we continue to deal with the difficulties and complications of her care and thankfully God has been faithful to help us keep our promise to her. I believe God has called me to do this and I trust Him in all these things.

I have come to believe in the power of prayer, and in intercession. I trust in my heart that He who has placed and deposited so much talent and skill in me, will in due time bring it to life for His praise and His glory. For those of you who have tried, hustled, and worked so hard to gain your footing but never seem to feel like you've accomplished what you set out to, don't worry. It's never a straight path to victory. Keep the faith! If you need faith, ask God for it. He is the author of our faith. We can't get true faith anywhere else. I encourage you to go straight to the source in prayer and be amazed. For every woman reading this today, I wish you all the love and all the joy in the world. Many blessings to you and yours. May God bless your dreams and the desires of your hearts.

CELIA GARCIA

Author, Speaker, Workshop Facilitator & International Career Coach

Over a span of 30 years, Celia Garcia has provided strong leadership and vision to tens of thousands of participants in over 40 programs. The programs have focused on delivering custom workforce development training, bridging the gap in services available to underserved minority communities, and the needs  of an aging workforce by improving job skills for Adult Learners and providing business training to Small Business Owners. She brings with her, wisdom and vast experience in serving the special needs of employers and their surrounding communities that continue to face huge workforce development challenges.

She has dedicated her career to establishing workplace literacy and job training programs which have delivered direct bilingual training services to generations of workers in an effort to improve the critical language skills and job skills required to improve performance on the job, identify potential career paths, and move low wage workers to qualify for and attain higher wages. She has also been instrumental in creating national partnerships with like-minded organizations dedicated to improving economic conditions for families by promoting self-sufficiency through workforce development initiatives and by teaching financial literacy to families struggling to get ahead in establishing and stabilizing their lives in the US.

She has recently completed two terms as State Deputy Director for Women for CA LULAC and is the Founder and Executive Director of the Latin Business Institute, a non-profit Community Based Organization that is dedicated to economic development through job skills and entrepreneurial training since 1997. She is also the CEO of MujerValiente™ and miCOACHmx™ College and Career Planning, private consulting and coaching businesses, working with and for the Latino community in educational and empowerment initiatives. Ms. Garcia is currently serving as a board member for a local Charter School and Community Development Corporation in Santa Ana, California. Recently, she has been elected to serve as a national board member of the National Association of Workforce Development Professionals and has the distinct privileged of representing the State of California with a personal focus on customized initiatives in the Southern California community. She is recognized for her work and holds a national certification as a Workforce Development Professional.

Ms. Garcia and miCOACHmx have partnered with state and federal government, private enterprise, post secondary institutions, and community organizations to address the job training needs of the immense workforce in Southern California and have developed a professional training institute and online services, combining valuable human resource expertise, skill building, creative tools, and professional development resources; all designed to develop the competitive edge needed by so many.

A LEADER IS SOMEONE WHO DEMONSTRATES WHAT IS POSSIBLE

My name is Maria Veronica Corona, yes "Maria" a name that I didn't know I had until I had to fill out my college application and I was asked for my legal name. I grew up being called Vero or Veronica, never Maria. I am the oldest of two brothers Jose and Gerry and one sister Elodia "Yoya." I am the proud daughter of Mexican immigrant parents that came here from Jalisco, Mexico for a better opportunity. They did their best to give us all they could and raised me to become the woman I am today, an Entrepreneur, Bilingual-Speaker, and Community Leader.

My parents instilled in me strong values, morals, hard work and dedication in all that I do. They worked very hard to give my brothers, sister, and I a better life; a life that they did not have, and always encouraged us to excel.

Wow, to think two young immigrants, with barely a high school education, came to this country almost 50 years ago, without knowing any English and raised me to be the woman I am today.

I am beyond words on my upbringing. The values instilled in me which have guided me in life through all the blessings and lessons, hardships and successes that I have overcome in my life and continue to guide me in being optimistic.

Growing up there was never any doubt that we were a Mexican, Catholic family. From the food we ate to the music we heard. Frijoles de la olla was always part of our meals and on occasion, handmade tortillas. Growing up, every meal was a homemade meal and having dinner as a family was normal. Sundays were my favorite day, going to church and eating out was fun, it was a luxury only done on Sundays. The crucifix and Virgen de Guadalupe image was always on display and I can't forget praying the rosary every night especially when our Abuelita Amalia came over. We also observed all the religious holidays. Today I am grateful for the beliefs and faith instilled in me, which have guided me to becoming a better person!

The music we listened to was mostly Spanish, Mariachi, Norteñas, romantic and of course, my favorite, cumbias. From Jose Alfredo Jimenez, Ramon Ayala, Lola Beltran, and Antonio Aguilar to Vicente Fernandez. I must admit, I didn't care to listen to this music then, and now it's part of my playlist.

I can't forget the Telenovelas, watched those also. We would gather around as a family to watch them. Those were fun times, we only had one TV, we all had to agree on what show we were going to watch. It was one of the several times we gathered together as a family aside from dinner.

Growing up at home we mostly spoke Spanish. Today, I am grateful to be bilingual and able to speak, read and write both Spanish and English. Being bilingual has really helped me be where I am today professionally. As much as I may not have liked the rules my parents instilled in me while growing up, today, I've learned to appreciate my culture and upbringing a lot more! Especially the value of hard work and dedication to providing for our family.

I went to public school, grew up with all the commodities, in a 3 bedroom, 2-bathroom house in the suburbs of Pacoima, CA with running water, electricity and food on our table, with frijoles de la olla always on the stove. We even had a live-in nanny who took care of us while our parents were working.

Growing up I always felt I was in charge; I had to be the perfect child to set the example for the rest of my siblings. I remember since a very young age having to translate for my parents, now I wonder, was I even translating correctly? I even handled the checkbook, only because I was the only one able to write a check. I realize now where my wanting to be in control comes from, since growing up I was in control.

In the past ten years of my journey of personal development, self-discovery, to a better version of myself, I have learned that I always pride myself on being intelligent, at times thinking I was better than everyone, a perfectionist. I have come to terms that I am not. I don't know everything and I am not better than anyone else. To discover this, I've had to learn to be vulnerable. This has not been easy. I have come to terms with my ego because she is arrogant and not always easy to deal with. I also learned that I'd rather be happy than be right!

I'm still a recovering perfectionist that can do everything on my own. I can't change who I am. However, I have learned to become present and aware of my way of being, especially letting go and asking for help.

Being the oldest, I was the first to have to experience many events in life, especially when it came to education. I remember my first day of school, I was excited to attend school, but I had no clue what to expect. I was just dropped off at my Kindergarten class. I remember just crying feeling abandoned.   All I can think of was, I am by myself and worried of who would take care of my brothers?

This experience made me the person I am today, with strong character and not afraid to face what comes my way. Because at the end all will work out for its highest good. Taking care of others, was just my preparation to becoming the leader I am today. I have learned the importance to love and take care of me first, before others.

All my life in school, I had many friends and was a good student in my class, always getting straight A's.   Even though I had many friends, I never did any extracurricular activities with them. I always had to go home to do my homework, help with homework, and do house chores.

It was not until my senior year that I was finally able to go to school dances and football games; I even made it to prom. I proudly attended San Fernando High School, home of the mighty Tigers ~ Class of 1986! During high school I had some fun times dancing and hanging out with my friends as well as my first job experience at El Pollo Loco.

I liked working. It gave me exposure to the public and I enjoyed dealing with people. I then moved up and worked at JC Penny's. This was even more fun; I got to dress up to go to work. I made more new friends and had a lot of admirers. In working with the public, I learned customer service and how to deal with different type of personalities. This was my preparation for my future career endeavors.

After graduating high school, I went out more with my friends, and I even had a boyfriend. I would go to house parties with my friends on Friday nights after our night shift working at UPS. I would tell my parents I was working late, when I was dancing the night away to what today is called old school music. It was the popular thing to do back in the 80's in the San Fernando Valley.

During this time, I was attending LA Valley College, it was not easy having to work, go to school, and do homework. However, I was always about excelling and doing my best. I was the first one in my family to go to college and all though I have a large extended family, no one had gone before me. I remember that once I was ready to transfer to a 4-year university, I was nervous and scared.

One of my counselors guided me on what to do. I also went to my first-grade teacher at Sharp Avenue school, who encouraged me to major in business administration. As well as my neighbor who was more than excited to help me fill out my college application for CSUN-Cal State Northridge and gave me a recommendation letter.

While I was excited to apply for college, I was now dealing with my dad wanting to move our family to the Central Coast, to become a Strawberry Farmer. I had worked harvesting strawberries during the summers in the past. It is not easy work getting up a the crack of dawn, working in the cold and wet fields. I remember my hands freezing and my pants being wet up to my knees from the plants as we walked into the strawberry fields to harvest the fruit. NO way! I am too "chica fresa" (posh) for that.

I recall my dad saying to my siblings and I, that if we did not get an education, this would be the type of work we would end up doing. I knew that I did not want to work the fields picking strawberries. I just enjoy eating them!

As my dad was moving the family to the Central Coast. I had to leverage the fact that he told us that if we wanted to go to school he would support us. Oh, and it really helped that I gave him the tour on campus. It only made him prouder that his daughter would be attending such a university.

I now finally felt independent, no longer in need of a chaperone to go out and now I was free to date. However, my focus was school and did not need the distractions or Lord forbid I get pregnant. So, I broke it off with my first boyfriend Max; the first young man I ever kissed! I really liked him, but I didn't want any distractions! I was determined to make my dad proud.

My dad had a hard time letting me go to school. Today, I understand he was only protecting me. He did not have a formal education; it was a lack of knowledge and fear of the unknown.

After graduating from college with a Bachelor's degree in Business. I moved to Santa Maria, CA. My dad had decided to continue being a farmer and would stay on the central coast. As much as I felt I can now conquer the world, since I was a college graduate, being the obedient daughter, I moved to the central coast. The truth was, my two jobs were not enough to support me to be on my own and too much of my dislike, off I went.

My mid-twenties were the roughest years of my life, many challenging moments that were very difficult. I lived in Santa Maria, CA for eight very long years. My mid 20's were not happy years; I did not like it there, it was about keeping up with the Joneses. Living there came with more responsibility. My dad having a farming business, had me doing payroll, paying the bills, and living in the farm town was not fun. You can take a girl out of the city, but you can take the city of angels out of the girl.

There I was in a small farm town, I had just graduated college, marriage had not crossed my mind. However, all my cousins and relatives were getting married. I felt completely out of place; suddenly, I felt the pressure of wanting to get married because everyone else was. The movie 28 Dresses has nothing on me. I was always the bridesmaid and never the bride. Although deep down inside, I felt I still had so much to do in life before taking this step. I finally started dating and ended up in a relationship that was toxic. As I have evolved, I believe it was a way of self-sabotage to not get married.

The best time of my life while living in the central coast were the three years I served as chair of the Hispanic Business Committee for the Santa Maria Chamber of Commerce. This was my first experience at giving back to my community and evolving in my leadership skills and its due to the great mentors I had.

My biggest accomplishment was helping develop a new event: "The Strawberry Recognition Dinner" where we would recognize local strawberries farmers. The three years, I served on the chamber, I developed my leadership skills, learned to organize events, and fundraise. I felt a sense of belonging for the first time; it was empowering to be part of my community. I had also created new relationships outside of my large family. Today I have the satisfaction of a great accomplishment; this recognition dinner grew from 50 people to what I hear is well over 1000 in attendance today. Little did I know that this was just the beginning of my preparation for bigger things to come into my life as a community leader.

While I had found my new sense of belonging the worst moment of my life occurred. Not in a million years would I had expected this. My parents separated! This was a big blow for me. How can this be happening? Why after 25 years of marriage!

The next five years were very difficult and very dark years for me. Once my dad was gone, I assumed I was in charge and took the role upon myself of being mom and dad. Those were dark years in my life: lots of pressure, no money to pay our bills. I felt there was no one to turn to. At the same time, I was still involved with the Chamber; it was the one thing that just kept me going and in a positive state of mind.

When you go through tough times and rough moments is when you find your true supporters. I will forever be grateful to the Cortez family, who are beyond friends; they are my family who have been very supportive in all that I do and there for me in the most challenging of times. Today, they continue being part of my life. I love them dearly!

While facing these difficult times and not being happy, I recall my friend Beverly whom was another very supportive person in my life. She encouraged me to do what was best for me and not be afraid to do what I wanted in life. She introduced me to the first glimpse of personal development by taking me to Zig Ziglar training whose special guest was John Maxwell. This changed my life and gave me a new-found courage!

This was when I made the decision to move back to the Los Angeles area. It was something I sincerely felt from the bottom of my heart I had to do. My brother Jose had just started a business, my brother Gerry had completed his four years of service in the Marines and my sister had just graduated high school. I felt like it was the right time to make a change. This was 19 years ago.

For the first time in my life, I was doing something I really wanted. I felt liberated. However uncertain of what would happen next. I loaded my car with my clothes, some personal belongings and said my goodbyes to my mom. As I drove onto the 101 Freeway after a moment of reflection I turned on the radio and I hear this song- "Give me a reason to stay here and I will turn myself around." I will never forget that moment. I distinctly remember it as if it just happened today. As I listened to the lyrics of this song I recall taking a deep breath knowing I was doing what was best for me. There was absolutely no reason to stay.

That moment confirmed that I had a new journey to explore in my life. Little did I know what an amazing journey it continues to be today. I have learned that we must face some dark moments and situations, before discovering who we really are. We must go through major breakdowns to have breakthroughs that will change our life. Understanding this has helped me face a new journey of the gift of life. The experience has been the joy in life!

Although I moved back to Los Angeles, where I felt at home, it was different. I did not return to the San Fernando Valley; I was now in Pico Rivera, a whole new area for me to explore. I was roommates with my cousin Yolanda, who was very supportive with my transition. I was happy to have a job and be back living in the city, but it wasn't fulfilling. I wanted more however, I was not sure what that more was.

I started my new job at Extra-Help, an employment agency that sent laborer workers to warehouse and factories in the City of Commerce and Vernon. I learned a new industry and how to deal with people from all social classes where my bilingual skills were very useful. I started in the payroll department and quickly moved my way up to recruiter, then dispatcher, then onsite manager for one of the company's largest accounts. This was my early 30's; I had a decent job. However, I felt mixed emotions, sometimes happy, sometimes depressed. I was going through many transitions in life. All I did was work and barely able to make ends meet. I really didn't have many friends and the few I did were an hour away. I was always the one making an effort to visit them and get together. Today, I understand how some friends are meant for life, for a reason and a season. They had been there for a season. As my life has transformed, I have learned that we must let go of the old to make room for the new.

That is when I reconnected with my friend Maricela, another supportive friend in my life. She reminded me of being in the present and enjoying life to the fullest. Grateful how she always found a way to bring out the best in me, even today after 25 years of unconditional friendship!

As I felt settled back into the city, I was content with my job and deep down inside knew something better would come my way and it did. I was hired by an established building maintenance company in Monterey Park and I am forever grateful for the opportunity of a lifetime.

Now I felt more established, working in a place that I really enjoyed. I felt happy and financially stable in my new career path. I was also dating and met several nice men. However, I didn't feel ready for marriage, at least not emotionally.

I have come to terms and accepted that not being married or having children was my choice, as difficult it was to accept, today I'm at peace with my choice. I do believe one day I will be married to a man that accepts me as I am and as I am not, will love and cherish me unconditionally.

As I continued to develop and evolve through my journey, I was growing in my new career. I really enjoyed my experience being a student of the janitorial industry, which has turned out to be very successful industry for me.

I am grateful for this experience of working my way up from Benefits Coordinator to Customer Service Manager. Then within three years promoted to Branch Manager and after four years in this position, due to stress, I transferred to Business Development/Sales.

I was the first employee in the company to be recognized in all the positions I held during my employment in this company. Not only the first employee, but one of the first few women in a male dominated industry.

I am proud of my accomplishments, however, all I did was work, work, and work! Although I enjoyed working for this company, and enjoyed life more, I was not entirely happy. I put work before family, friends and most importantly myself. I worked so much and had so much stress that one day I drove myself to the hospital thinking I had a heart attack; crazy, right? I remember I could not breathe. It turned out I was having an anxiety attack. In my follow-up appointment, my doctor suggested to change my lifestyle because I was not getting enough sleep. I was under so much stress and I realized I was hiding at work by working 10-12 hours per day because I was not happy. I had very little balance in my life and now I needed to take care of my health. This was a turning point!

After my anxiety attack incident, I changed positions at work and was now doing business development, less stressful and more fun. I also embarked on a new spiritual journey and met Silvia and Susan, who have been great friends since.

It was an amazing experience and really helped let go of all the guilt and resentment I had. I forgave others and most importantly myself. I learned to be at peace, become empathetic, more loving, and compassionate towards others and especially myself.   This was just the beginning of creating more balance in my life. I was earning good money, I had financial stability and enjoying life more.   I was enjoying time with family and friends, going out more, dating and traveling. Most importantly finding joy in life.

During this time, I had another supportive friend, Elisa, who encouraged me to travel and joined me on my dating quest in search of finding a good man... boy do we have some interesting dating stories! I'm very grateful to her for always pulling me out of work to do something fun, which included dancing the night away.

While enjoying myself, and creating a balanced life with family, friends, work, and fun; a new opportunity came my way. I received a generous job offer as general manager to oversee the west coast operations for another janitorial company based in the East Coast. It took me several sleepless nights to think this offer over. After nine and a half years, I made the decision to leave my employer. It was not an easy decision. However, I was ready for a new adventure in my life.

I started working for my new employer, he had made me an offer I could not refuse. I was excited to be earning more money, start saving, living in a nice home and driving a luxury car.   After only a few months, I realized I started sacrificing my lifestyle again. I was working long hours and my values were not aligned with my latest employer. After a year and a half I decided to resign.

Spiritually and emotionally, I was in a good place, resigning came easy. I felt fearless and my decision became very clear no matter how much money I was earning, it was not worth sacrificing my happiness.

Upon my resignation, I received a call from a customer to inform me about the possibility of a new cleaning contract. My jaw dropped, I had just resigned! I asked to meet with her and explained what had happened. On my way to meet her, I called my friend Mauricio, we worked together at the time. He encouraged me that I needed to go out on my own and suggested I start my own business. However, I was not sure that is what I wanted.

I met with my customer and explained to her what was happening; what she said to me next completely changed my life. She saw something in me that I had not seen in myself, she said "I am only giving you this building because of you, I don't even like your boss!". That gave me a boost of confidence and before I knew it, I asked her to give me an opportunity, she did and I embarked on the journey of entrepreneurship. I have now been in the business of "Keeping it Clean while you Sleep" for the past 8 years with my business partner, Mauricio. I'm very grateful to my first customer, Romy, for believing in me.

I ventured into entrepreneurship and went from earning six figures, to no figures, to not knowing when I was going to get paid. What drives my passion? My customers that believe in me and my loyal and hardworking employees. It has not been an easy journey and if I had to do it all over again, I would.

Our business continues to grow due to our passion, hard work, dedication, and many sacrifices. Thank you, Mauricio for your encouragement!

I was now an entrepreneur and uncertain if this new journey was for me when I received a call from Rose, a friend, who introduced me to the National Latina Business Women Association Los Angeles (NLBWA-LA).

She invited me to attend a new program they were launching, the 2010 Business Management Academy. Little did she know that I was undecided if I wanted to be in business. I still decided to show up with an open mind and was intrigued during the first session. By the time I walked out of the first session, I was inspired and encouraged by the passion of the 35 fellow entrepreneurs.

Joining this six week program embarked me into a new phase of leadership that changed my life. I joined NLBWA-LA board of directors and eventually became President, serving a 2-year term from 2012 to 2014. Grateful, proud, and honored for this opportunity of a new mission in life to inspire, empower and support fellow Latina women entrepreneurs. I am beyond grateful for evolving as a leader in my community and for all the phenomenal people that I have met and the countless opportunities that have come my way. I truly believe that the more you give the more you receive. Being part of my community and giving back has given me much more than I could have ever asked for. Today, I feel more at peace, living in gratitude and happier.

Being humble, while learning and evolving in this journey of life, I am grateful for my upbringing, my challenges, and opportunities. It continues to be an amazing journey of self-discovery and being aware of this only makes me stronger and more compassionate towards myself. To be a better daughter, sister, Tia, friend, leader, business woman and eventually wife.

My mission in life is to continue in my journey of self-discovery, be my true authentic self, stay grateful and surprised by the joys of life. My purpose and legacy is to be compassionate, loving, and a genuine woman. To follow my core values, give back, empower, and inspire others in life.

As leaders, we are world changers. To be a mindful leader, practice self-observation without judgment by focusing on the present, having a clear mind and focusing on what's important. Be creative and find joy in all that you do.

Always follow your passion and believe in yourself!

To my biggest cheerleader my mom, Elodia Chavez, gracias mom por todo su apoyo y amor! La quiero mucho. And to my Corona Family, I love you!

VERONICA CORONA

Veronica Corona works hard to keep it clean in Southern California office buildings. In fact, "Keeping It Clean While You Sleep" is the motto of her company, CM Cleaning Solutions, a world-class janitorial services firm headquartered in Los Angeles, CA. As the owner and managing partner of one the area's leading commercial cleaning businesses, she believes a clean building or office space is a true testament to a company's branding and level of customer care. Her clients clearly agree.

The CM Cleaning Solutions client list includes some of the top corporations in the country like Warner Bros., Entrepreneur Media, Community Bank, and Vanir Development Company, to name a few.

Prior to starting CM Cleaning Solutions, she managed a janitorial company in Los Angeles, where she achieved over $1 Million in sales for two consecutive years. She later went on to work for another company where a customer encouraged her to start her own business. In 2009, she and her business partner did just that. With a lot of hard work, the two have grown the company to a million-dollar business in less than five years.

A 15-year veteran of the commercial janitorial service industry, Veronica is committed to providing personalized service. She is even known to roll up her sleeves and join a crew to ensure client satisfaction.

She attributes her drive and dedication to her parents whom emigrated to the U.S. from Mexico and instilled a strong work ethic in Veronica and her three siblings. That work ethic combined with a passion for fostering relationships has led her to become an award-winning entrepreneur. She has been recognized by the California Hispanic Chamber of Commerce as a Rising Star in 2015 , recognized as Mujer Destacada by La Opinion in 2013, honored with the 2014 Latina of Influence award by Hispanic Lifestyles magazine, and she was presented with the 2014 Small Business Award by the Los Angeles Latino Chamber of Commerce.

With a strong desire to give back and to empower and inspire women, the bilingual Los Angeles native is active in her community and serves on the boards of several non-profits, including the California Hispanic Chamber of Commerce, National Latina Business Women Association (NLWBA) as advisor, Financially Fit Foundation and HBN Bilingual Toastmasters. She is also past president of NLWBA Los Angeles and a Competent Communicator in Toastmasters

Her passion is to make a difference in others' lives and journey to success, by always leading in her true authentic leadership style and being a graceful and genuine woman! She believes that as leaders, we are world changers.

When Veronica is not managing day-to-day operations of CM Cleaning Solutions, volunteering or speaking, you can find her perfecting her swing at a local golf course, reading or spending time with her family and friends.

PERFECTLY IMPERFECT

In my life, things have always seemed to happen to me on their own timing, and opportunities have come up that I could have never imagined possible. The chance to guide others and to be recognized, that I have inspired someone and have worked just hard enough for someone else to notice. It seems that these opportunities have come at the most inopportune times for me. Times when I am going through a struggle or when it seems that things are not going exactly the way I planned. That's when the universe steps in to remind and assure me that I am on the right path.

Once Again, thank you to the universe for allowing me to contribute to this amazing collaboration. I am humbled and honored to know that I will be part of something so much greater than myself, and that I can share my story with other women who are also committed to inspire, who are always striving to be better, and who want to make this world a better place. To the women who share a mutual passion for creating a community of support, not only for Latina women, but for all women in our pursuit of happiness.

My only wish for this project is that someone can relate with my story, with my experiences and my struggles, and in some way, they find the inspiration they need for their personal breakthrough. It is not the greatest story ever told or a story about how many houses I've sold or how wonderful and perfect my life is. On the contrary, it is a story of hardships and struggles but also triumphs through hard times, and I am humbled to share it with you.

> "Alone we can make a difference-together we can change the world." —Irina Bokov, director-general UNESCO

MY ROOTS

I am first generation, born in Chicago, Illinois, and the oldest of four. My parents emigrated from northern Mexico, looking for what most immigrants come to the United States for: the American dream, the opportunity to pursue a better life for their children and to live in a country that allows them to be safe and free.

Our upbringing was peaceful, and although our parents worked a lot, there was never a time they left us alone. They worked hard. I never heard them complain about anything and I always saw them do the best they could without ever asking anyone for help. My mother and father were both factory workers and worked opposite schedules to make sure that someone was always home. They made sure that we grew up in a safe neighborhood, regardless of the extra sacrifice that it took to live in a better area. Growing up, I would slowly learn the challenges that my father faced, including being deported several times, and continuing to come back, time after time. I did not really understand until I got older the sacrifices he made, but I knew that we were in the land of opportunity and that there were no limitations on what I could do.

I started working with my mother at the early age of 14 on a worker's permit in her factory. She was the second-shift, night manager, and I was so blessed that I had the opportunity to work with her and see the amazing leader she was. She was a boss and an entrepreneur. She always found a way to make additional income, whether it was selling clothes, jewelry, or basically anything she could make a profit on. I admired her and her confidence. She was tough, but respected, and I always found that to be endearing.

Since I can remember, from a young age I have always had the passion to help. I wanted to "change the world, to end world poverty and hunger!" Yes, that was me. I was on a mission, and no one could tell me otherwise. There was no doubt in my mind what I would go to school for or what my personal goals entailed. I received my bachelor's degree in behavioral sciences from National Lewis University and immediately began to work for the Illinois Department of Children and Family Services as a case manager for foster children.

My caseload consisted of children who were in the foster care system, some for years, due to various forms of emotional, physical, and sexual abuse. It was an extremely emotional job and a time when I learned to really understand societal problems and how it contributes directly to the inequality in our communities.

Witnessing the pattern of abuse, from generation to generation, and the vicious cycle of violence, gave me an even greater empathy and understanding of people. Our values start at home. When we are taken care of and loved, we reciprocate that joy. When we receive anger and hate, we reciprocate those feelings as well.

My plans were to get my master's degree in child psychology and pursue my career further but God had another plan for me.

LEARNING TO BE AN ENTREPRENEUR

During my time working with foster youth, I obtained my real estate license; when I randomly took a real estate course with a friend getting into the business.

Well, I was not a natural entrepreneur, unlike my mother. Real estate would have never been my first career choice. I didn't imagine myself selling anything, let alone one of the largest, tangible purchases of one's life. I started selling part-time and before I knew it, I began to make a career from it. My passion and purpose has always been to serve others, but I also knew that this would allow me the opportunity to pursue my dreams and make enough money to truly give back. I decided to enter the real estate world full-time, and my career began.

The realities of living the entrepreneur life: the rejection, the hustle, the competition, and trying to get ahead in the market were shocking to me. I struggled the first few years to have a consistent income, because I never had the guidance, help, and mentorship, which you need in this profession. The problem was that I simply did not know what I needed to know.

I would go on to practice for 17 years, and although the rollercoaster life of a salesperson has not been an easy one, it is the hardest job I have ever loved! The struggles of this business have been overcome by the work I have done and the relationships that I have created with the families that trusted me to guide them in such a significant time in their lives.

MY CRASH!

In 2005, at the peak of the real estate market when I had finally been able to create a business for myself, I fell into a deep depression. Financially, it was the most money I had made at that point, yet no amount of money could ever prevent what I would go on to experience. The type of depression I had, I had only studied and read about in textbooks, and it was completely debilitating. I was prescribed medication that was supposed to help me get better. Instead, I experienced severe side effects that triggered my anxiety disorder.

It was the most unlikely of times, but that is when I met my husband. I was in a deep depression and I wanted nothing to do with myself, let alone anyone else. At that time, I knew that taking medication was not going to be an option for me, so my journey would begin in understanding how to get better and how to find the relief that I desperately needed in other ways. When things were dark and there was little hope, once again God was by my side and sent me the man who would become my husband and my saving grace.

For a long time, I was ashamed and embarrassed about what I was dealing with. Few people knew. At that time, mental illness was not a topic openly discussed, and I remember thinking how horrible it was that people were on medication to be able to cope. Now there is more of an understanding and less of a stigma about the issue, and only recently, I've been more open with my story about this ongoing struggle. Dealing with depression and anxiety is not something you want to openly share with someone. It is not easy to admit especially when we as women tend to keep everything inside while still managing to work a full day, run a household, and keep it all together.

WRONG PLACE AT THE RIGHT TIME?

It was in November 2007, when along with the complete downturn of the financial and economic market, my business collapsed right before my eyes. Still dealing with my ongoing health issues, it would just be another obstacle that I would go through and yet another chapter in my life. At the time, I did not know, but this was one of the best things that could have ever happened to me.

I was in survival mode. There came that point in time that I needed to decide whether to get a full-time job somewhere else, and jobs were scarce at the time, or continue to follow the profession that I loved so much. I knew that the *only* way that I would survive in this field was by learning how to adapt and learning to work in a completely distressed and volatile market.

I was completely broke, living paycheck to paycheck, and making minimum wage when I asked my mother to cosign a loan for me. I invested in real estate education that taught me more than buying and selling but the skills necessary to be able to reinvent myself through real estate. I had to take a chance and bet on myself, believe that I was good at what I did, and that I had the skillset and determination to not give up.

It was not overnight that I started to make money again, but it was here that I would meet the people who would inspire me and become my first mentors. This was where my mind would be opened and where I would become in tune with who I was. I would realize something critical, that what I had always been missing was mindset. That I could change my circumstances just by changing my thoughts, and that if I wanted things to be better, I needed to be better. That it was not about what happened to us, but our attitude and reaction towards it. Once I started to really understand this, I was also able to understand and control my emotions and began to get a better handle and understanding of my anxiety.

In 2008, I took the last of my real estate classes in Arizona and barely made it back home, because I could not pay the $25 fee to check my bag. I had hit that "rock bottom" everyone talks about, at the airport, in the women's bathroom on the floor, crying uncontrollably.

Just one week after coming home from that experience, my partner and I ended up wholesaling a property with no money and no credit. We made a profit of nine-thousand dollars in one day. This was what sparked our rise, and before we knew it, we were running a full-scale, professional, loss mitigation company that would go on to help hundreds of families in active foreclosure. We went on to negotiate and settle millions of dollars in overvalued debt with lenders across the country and helped families avoid foreclosure, settle their debt, or be able to keep their home. This was proof that my coursework, confidence in myself, and financial gamble had started to pay off.

We worked twenty-four hour days creating a business that never existed, building systems that we needed to be able to handle the volume, and just trying to figure out how we could make it all work. The banks were saturated with short sales and there was a lack of resources to help handle that type of unprecedented volume. We learned as we went, and many times would end up working for free. Nevertheless, we went on to be recognized for our work with various organizations, publications, and served on a panel with Fannie Mae, Freddie Mac, and major lenders across the country discussing our experiences. We had many encounters with asset managers and negotiators and ultimately became a resource for attorneys as well as outside realtors and colleagues.

We spoke all over the city, including the Chicago Public Schools, educating families and providing resources for them to find out what their options were. Although it was a difficult job, both professionally and emotionally, I was always grateful to God that once again He gave me the opportunity to help others by doing what I loved to do.

We were committed to do what we could in helping to stabilize and rebuild communities affected by the foreclosure epidemic through education and service, no matter how small the impact. For us, it truly was about helping families navigate through a challenging time and on to the next phase in their lives.

Throughout this period, we rehabbed and wholesaled our own projects and began working with investors, rehabbers, private and hard-money lenders, while learning the various ins and outs of real-estate investing.

At that time, being able to work alongside successful investors was incredibly rewarding and empowering because our efforts were predominately led by women.

> "The road to success and the road to failure are almost exactly the same." —Colin R. Davis

In 2014, I was recognized by the National Association of Hispanic Real Estate Professionals (NAHREP) for consecutively being in the Top 250 Realtors across the country. I was personally invited to go to Los Angeles for the NAHREP annual conference and be honored.

It was at this event where I would have the pleasure of meeting Nely Galan, real estate entrepreneur, media mogul, and women's advocate. She was one of the first in her industry to rise to the top and a pioneer in women empowerment. She was on stage talking about the incredible opportunities available in today's world for Latina women. She spoke about how we were the largest emerging market, the "sleeping giant" in America and that the opportunities that were before us would be life-changing. She said there was no greater time in history to be a woman and that it was time for us to step up and take on leadership roles that could empower others to do the same.

She made me change the way I looked at myself and my abilities and taught me that I had something to share with others. I accepted that I could also be the mentor that I never had.

I was transfixed by her passion and her determination to empower women. She spoke passionately about the importance of stepping up and taking leadership roles within our circles where we could create that community and embrace that we are agents of change because our voices mattered. That it would be our responsibility to be leaders for this generation of young women and teach our daughters the power in our abilities and that there are no limitations.

Before that experience, it had taken me a long time not to judge myself through someone else's eyes. However, I realized that I had more strength than I thought and that I had taken the initiative to never quit. I realized that I did it without the mentors, the personal development, the support, or any kind of a professional foundation. I did it on my own and, despite everything, I succeeded.

We must be proud of the things we are able to do because only we can understand the strength that it took.

Through this experience and as my affiliations with other organizations developed, I have been able to meet the most amazing women throughout the country.

Our stories are all very similar. We all have had challenges: we all have suffered; and we followed our dreams despite it. I learned that we are all looking for the same opportunities to provide for our families. We all want to set an example for our daughters to aspire to become great in whatever path they may choose.

As women, we can be anything we want to be. We have the tools and resources, now more than ever. Most of all we have the passion, the drive, and the determination.

"Before you can be chosen, you need to choose yourself first."

—Nely Galan, Self-Made Leadership

LEADERSHIP

I have always been driven by my own principles, to stay true to myself, and to always follow my heart. Success for me has never been defined by money. I always believed in working hard, being honest, and sincerely taking care of others and their best interests. I loved working for myself and having the freedom to focus on my own business, but I also knew that there was more for me.

After owning my own successful brokerage for almost 15 years, I was offered a position with an up and coming real estate company with core values that aligned with my personal vision of philanthropy, community, and support. I decided to once again take the leap of faith. It was not an easy decision and if you would have told me at the time that I would be closing the doors to my beloved company that I worked so hard for, I would have told you that you were crazy.

However, I knew that it would be an opportunity for me to grow as a leader while being able to give back not only my resources, but my time to share what I have learned through leadership and inspiration with my newly found empowerment. I knew that God would always lead me in the right direction, even though the roads have not always been paved.

It has been an incredible journey thus far seeing the company grow so quickly and attract likeminded people with the same passion and energy to make a difference and pay it forward.

For me, it is about investing my time to help others achieve their goals, sharing my experiences, and being the mentor that I never had. I believe that effective leadership is about understanding one's differences and learning from one another and help each other grow.

> "If your actions inspire others to dream more, learn more, do more and become more, you are a leader."
> —John Quincy Adams, former US President

GIVING BACK

I believe that giving back is one of the most important things that we can do. Being successful in today's world is essential, but being successful comes with a great responsibility to provide for others.

The more I dedicate my time to community service, the more giving back becomes part of me. It is a part of who I am and I am thankful to God that I can do so. It does not matter if you donate money or time and you don't have to be rich to make a difference.

If we can just stop for a minute and try to see the world through someone else's life and think a little, then we can have a deeper understanding of one another.

Success is not only about money; true success begins the second that you start to give and when you love what you do, the money comes.

> "Don't tell me how much money you make, but what you do to make a difference in your community."
> —Eduardo Garcia, CEO Realty of Chicago

INSPIRATION

"Be yourself, everyone else is already taken."

—Oscar Wilde, Irish essayist

When I was asked to collaborate on this book, of course I thought, *Why me?* Right. It's that self-doubt that we burden ourselves with instead of just being thankful and receiving it. It's the fear of failure, that I am not accomplished enough, successful enough, strong enough, and pretty enough. You know, "the story" that we tell ourselves.

I must have quit 100 times before I even started, constantly questioning what worth I would bring to this book. It is so easy for us to measure ourselves against others or to search for ourselves in others. It's the pressure to conform to be the person who others want you to be, and I have done it many times in my life.

Self-doubt is exactly what stops us from moving forward and taking chances. I easily could have chosen to pass on this opportunity because of my doubts, but I didn't. I knew that it was not by accident that I was asked to collaborate and with that I understood the great responsibility to share my story.

There have been a lot of challenges, and living with anxiety has tested me more than anything else in my life, but no matter what, I have always bet on myself. Many times, it was physically painful to work and to keep focused on business, but my work has also been a source of relief and therapy for me.

Sometimes when I stand back and really focus on my accomplishments and not my failures, I wonder, "How in the world did I do that? How did I have the strength?"

I have taken many chances and have failed miserably over and over again. However, the toughest experiences in my life have been those that I have learned from the most and the direct contributing factor to where I am today and where I am going. That bumpy road that we sometimes find ourselves on is the *only* road designed for you that will take you to your personal destination.

"When you feel like giving up, remember why you held on for so long in the first place." —Unknown

If you are reading this book, it is because you are searching for something, because you want something better, because you know that your intentions and goals are attainable.

We do not choose our circumstances, our families, or our socio-economic status. But one thing that we always have is the ability to dictate our own lives. We choose to take the chances that we need to, in order to follow our dreams. Focus on the positive things in your life and align yourself with women who empower you and who you look up to and most of all believe in you. Be proud of who you are!

I look forward to continuing to grow as a person, an entrepreneur and a mindful leader. I am so grateful that I have an incredible network and the support of hundreds of women who surround me, encourage me, and continue to inspire me every day.

There is only one you, one perfect beautiful you, made in the image of God.

God is within her, she will not fail —Psalm 46:5

DEDICATION

First and foremost, I want to thank God for his amazing grace and love and for allowing me this opportunity.

I have been blessed with the most wonderful family and friends anyone could ever ask for. Their unconditional support and love has been the greatest treasure in my life.

This is especially dedicated to my father, my mother, Jesus, and Jovita Antillon. For all the love and sacrifice that you have given us always, never let us go without, and being the best example of what a person should be.

To my mother, my everything, and the funniest person I know. I will never know what I did to deserve you. Thank you for always making sure to remind me of my worth and the beauty that I possess inside, no matter what my flaws.

To my wonderful husband, Tony, who has been on this rollercoaster ride with me and who has held me back every time I wanted to jump off. I am glad you are on this journey with me, and thank you for always believing in me more than I believed in myself. I would not be here without you!

Lastly, to my Sofi. She is the light of my life, my heart, and my soul. This book and everything I do is for you. Always know that God is with you and as long as you want, you can accomplish anything your little heart desires.

MAGGIE ANTILLON-MATHEWS

Maggie Antillon–Mathews lives in Chicago, Illinois, with her husband Tony and their 5-year-old daughter Sofia.

Maggie has been practicing real estate for the last 17 years and after owning her own brokerage for almost 15 years, she took on a new position as Managing Broker with Realty of Chicago, where she is in a leadership role and is a trainer and speaker. In just the first year and a half, Realty of Chicago has tripled their agent count and was named one of the top 20 growing real estate companies in Chicago. With Realty of Chicago's high recruitment of women, Maggie is committed to empowerment by teaching what she has learned to others.

She is passionate about what she does and has chosen to use her experiences to mentor others. She contributes her time and resources to charity and doing what she can to support her community. She belongs to the women's counsel of realtors, National Association of Hispanic Real Estate Professionals (NAHREP) and involved with various community organizations.

Maggie is excited about what the future holds with Realty of Chicago as a company that focuses on philanthropy, leadership and community. "I want to make sure our business grows with the right people who have the same vision as we do". "I am grateful to have the ability to use what I do to be able to give back. It's ingrained in me to try to make this world a better place."

THE TRANSFORMATIONAL CHALLENGE

My death bed "La Muerte" Ella y Yo—well, let's say -- we have had a close relationship. The closest. The darkest, deepest cataclysm of my heart's desires. The moments my heart stopped beating and every second of my dreams and yearnings hoping not to die, or better yet wishing lightning would strike and kill me instantly to stop reliving and feeling pain! Disillusion. The thoughts in my mind, while my health repeatedly relapsed and my life was in danger, these questions constantly racing in my head:

Why? ¿Para qué? Help? Why care? Who am I? Why am I here? What is needed of me at this stage? ¿Otra vez?

*What should I do with all this passion, creativity, and commitment that I feel in my heart needs to become a reality? I thought I had learned the lesson. What now? **Dios mío,** take me or leave me, but do it now!*

*__Estoy intentando__ to stay focused and in faith that better days are coming, but all this torture has me closing off to the universe and the world around me. Sinking in my sorrow, tears, **y mi sangre**. In my despair and while losing touch with reality, I visited my funeral in my heightened state of a medicated mind . . . I could vividly see my body going into a black hole. I mourned me in dreams and between states of sleep and medication. I couldn't breathe, and at times I wished to live, and other times I wished it would just stop! (I wasn't even 30 years old!)*

(Journal entries 2009-2016)

Yes, this was my experience while I was working diligently to build my life, dreams, skills in leadership, singing, entrepreneurial destiny, professional career, and so much more. I was forced to come to a complete halt, not once, but three times due to near-death experiences caused by complications of being diagnosed with polycystic ovarian syndrome (PCOS), a hormonal imbalance that affects 1 out of 10 women and can start in girls as young as 11 years old. It often goes undiagnosed until women have developed other health issues, such as diabetes, heart problems, and ovarian cancer.

This shook me to my core and made me question and reevaluate my goals and everything I knew, dreamed, and followed. Before this experience, I had built an immense connection to helping others, as well as being taught about business entrepreneurial spirit of my family. It was also instilled in me the responsibility we as humans must have to be helpful to one another, particularly to those in extreme need. Up to this point, I had devoted my life, academics, and career to help advocate for others and help heal communities havocked by violence and poverty.

I had become an expert in gender issues, human trafficking, violence prevention, diversity strategist, policy, social justice, and other topics. However, it was the lack of mindful leadership that I found even in the social, government, corporate, and nonprofit sectors in combination with my entrepreneurial upbringing that sent me back to the path of business and economic empowerment. Yet, I did not believe business had to be all about the "bottom line."

My goal was to find a balance! And when catastrophe struck my life, I was forced to practice what I preached. I could die today. *Had I met my mission and helped those I was supposed to reach? If I was so unhappy with what I found in the professional arena and the world, how could I influence change? What lessons did I learn from all my experiences and how could I help transform my life and that of others?*

LEADERSHIP AND YOUR MISSION

Becoming a leader in any field requires faith, discipline, sacrifice, determination, passion, compassion, connection, vision, love, balance, lessons, action, resistance, patience, strategy, work, failure, excitement, resilience, constant education, and more. But overall, it requires the ability to transform all the experiences into a positive reality for yourself and others. My journey to this point has made it clear—I must be ready for the unexpected and show my resilience. Therefore, I know I am meant to share my story for those who are ready to give up, but know in their hearts they have so much more to offer this world and those they love. More importantly, I want to give a glimpse as to what I learned about leading and giving back, despite the adversity, self-evaluation, rebirth, applying the lessons, and doing it all over again until it is my time to go. These changes and chaos were calling me to be present and more mindful as a business leader, lead singer, and advocate.

I feel that life has more significance than our routines and what we vociferously define as "normal." I understand that the most important thing for me is to connect with others and to be considerate of their needs and motivations. Plus, being born and raised in San Francisco, one of the most progressive and diverse places in the world, aside from its many imperfections, I discovered from observing my many mentors, and experiencing examples to recognize beauty in others first, be accepting of other's stories and truths as much as possible, and not to be judgmental. I learned to have open dialogue about opposing views and find shared goals. Be passionate about life and its diversity. Have a vision and realize that life does not revolve around me and only one path. Life on this planet is far beyond our small ideas and our own bubbles.

Early on, diversity, advocacy, and constant change surrounded me. I was exposed to people in need. There was no confusion in my mind that what we do as individuals, companies, societies, and countries impact us all! My parents, who emigrated from El Salvador, never let me forget how important it was to help others (as they had experienced poverty and need). School teachings made sure that we all knew we were a global community, from multicultural music exposure to showing me how to lead in conflict resolution. I never forgot these lessons, even when at different stages and travels I was the one attacked for being different.

I evidently knew where I stood. I knew that building a connection with others, showing leadership, and demonstrating compassion negotiated my spaces, reactions, interactions, and the likelihood of success. I want to be clear, success to me has never been measured only by finances and power, although these are important and not to be ignored. What it does mean for me is creating sustainable abundance while serving others and making broader changes and alignment of thought to the vision and values for those involved.

MY HISTORY AND THE CHALLENGE TO TRANSFORM

Let me share a condensed version of my initial entrepreneurial journey at a stage of total personal loss. (Note: this part of my story requires a book on its own—maybe someday I'll be ready to write it.) Although I had a form of a business and freelance service since the age of 13, my translations, corporate social responsibility, public affairs and diversity consulting business became official by getting my first business license when I turned 24, right before my health completely collapsed.

My personal life catastrophe was my health, and even though there was so much good and many opportunities around me, I was forced to stop. There were also an excessive number of situations and people who were wrong or eventually turned negative, influenced by the circumstances surrounding me, that prevented me from being myself. What was I going to do? I not only had to care for myself, but I was a major support for my parents, brother, extended family, community, and staff.

A year in, I had just turned 25; I should have had the world ahead of me. I already had done the leg work to be a community leader, entrepreneur, performer, coach, and public personality, but now I was unable to fully execute on what I had learned and was so eager to launch.

After this ordeal, I felt that there was no way that this was "going to be it." I felt inside I was meant to continue to make an impact on my local community and globally. I had survived to tell a story to help others find their voice and empowerment when everything else fails or self-destructs. I do not doubt that despite these near-death experiences, I always had a conscious and profound connection to working and giving the best to the causes and my work. By the age of 24, I had already coached, educated, and advocated for thousands of people, mostly women, and children. Here I was being given one of life's ultimate tests—multiple times. The message was clear: "Roxana, you have not **completed** your missions so go within and start working on your 5R's of transformation:

- Reevaluate

- Recalculate

- Reboot

- Rebirth

- Relaunch

(More information about the 5R's of Transformation can be found at www.empoderate.soy)

AWAKENING THE SPIRIT TO INFLUENCE CHANGE

I never learned to follow the status quo if I did not like something or a situation seemed unjust. I was always ready to question it, stand up for what I believed in, and do something about it. I could not understand why others did not feel the same way and sat quietly just taking it and doing nothing. This way of being, of course, got me into a lot of trouble growing up. Now, granted, there is always a time, place, and a need for a strategy to do something effectively (something I learned later in life), plus it is imperative to lead. Especially as women of color who have multiple differences with the mainstream American world, we must be strategic with our actions and messages, and we must choose our battles in order to be successful.

Back to my point of influencing change, after all is said and done, some things will never change, because no one steps up to create that change, no matter how small the change might be. For example, what if your neighbors on both sides are beating their spouses, and everyone looks the other way and acts as if nothing happened? The usual response is that's just the way it is. This example never settled well with me as a child. What do you mean that is what happens? At age 11, I would usually follow up with, "Did you not hear the terror, screaming, and pleading, or am I crazy to feel this is wrong?" As soon as the opportunity came up, I would find the way to connect with this person and offer help or at least let them vent. I often found people needed to be heard, and once this was done, they would usually also look for help. All it took was someone to care enough and act on it.

As I grew older, being careful to consider other's thoughts and experiences to influence change became instrumental. It was the establishment of this connection that allowed me to open doors, have access to discussions and results others could not have as easily as I did because of my experience working with sexual assault survivors to going to work in Rwanda and Uganda. Not to mention that my greatest form of creating a connection with any population was through my art and music. As a singer, I could help break down barriers and begin to open a space for education and dialogue to implement potential change. At the least, the music would spark a conversation and thought.

Connection and self-evaluation are two elements to consider as you aspire to influence change in any space. The questions are, "What are you bringing to the table and how are you presenting yourself?" I do not know where your soul is, but I can feel it when we arrive in a room. I feel the intention, and the energy, when we thrive and when we clash. What you bring to the room, the way you present yourself, how connected or disconnected in the space you are in—shows. I am not talking about what you are wearing, your gender, or your race. I am not speaking about what is visible.

I am speaking about the intangible, yet so ever-present, understanding that the people in front and back and around me are an engaged part of the mission we meet collectively to lead. Influencing change requires you to be present; having a coaching session with a client or staff demands your full and active attention. It is a form of mutual respect. No doubt, it is often said that good leaders are also great active listeners, and it shows in their results.

Creating influence and change not only happens slowly in the broader social, business, financial, and political worlds. It is a slow part of your personal journey. Influence and change in my world means focused strategy, innovation, disruption, creativity, and thinking outside the box using advocacy and negotiating skills. This means it is best that you have a full grasp of your topic, facts, and research well before trying to influence change.

INFLUENCING CHANGE AND THRIVING AFTER PERSONAL LOSS

The importance of this was tested and proven as my health deteriorated. I became a guinea pig for studies and after nine months of excruciating, nonstop hemorrhaging doctors turned me way saying that I had to accept this as my normal pattern. The medication provided made me worse, and I hardly found peace, even in prayer. Per some experts, I had an extreme case of PCOS, and it took me many trips abroad, thousands of dollars spent, and an infinite number of doctors, clinics, healers, meditation, surgeries, treatments, pills, herbs, needles, detox, and, of course, prayers to become whole and balanced again. The options were that I could either bleed to death; survive and due to the illness have a high potential for developing other high-risk health issues, or take immediate action to save my life! I went from feeling like Joan of Arc to Frida Kahlo's endless creative suffering. It suddenly became clear that this girl, me, who many believed had a promising future—who started college at 16, touring, singing, and advocate—might not make it.

With this potential horrific outcome, I had to become my strongest advocate. My history and experience with helping others, I now had to do for myself so that I could go up against "the experts." If it was up to them, I would be 6 feet under and not writing this chapter. I became the most knowledgeable person I knew on this topic. I befriended doctors, devoured research and information on the subject, and I spoke up for myself. I listened to my body and what it needed. I would not take no for an answer.

So, every time I hit another roadblock or medical setback, I asked myself, "Have I met my mission? I do not like what I see in this medical process so what am I doing to advocate change for myself and others?" I made it a point to educate every doctor, medical practitioner, and other people impacted by PCOS about me, my story, and what I had learned. I also listened to their knowledge and stories. I advocated for myself and have made sure to become involved in healthcare, PCOS education/advocacy globally, and launched the SOP International Association (www. alquimiaglobal.org).

As I navigated this challenging survival task, I also focused on coaching my clients, interns, audiences, and staff on being their best advocates by being and feeling empowered and not settling when a door closes, or they hear a negative answer. No was a nonnegotiable term in my world. Accepting a no meant I could lose my life. Is that the best I could do for me and for others? For doctors who turned me away, was this the best they could offer the thousands of women being impacted by PCOS globally? I could not sit around and wait for them, and I began my commitment to raise my voice on the topic. This, of course, not only applies to issues with my health, but it also applies to every area of life, and as a leader, I want to ensure that I am at least listening and finding alternatives for the many situations that those in leadership/decision positions face.

LESSONS LEARNED AND EXPERIENCES THAT SHAPE TRANSFORMATION

Catastrophes are inevitable, but how you deal with them is your choice. I heard this countless times as I found myself on the floor begging the universe to make the pain and bleeding go away. I had a choice to lay there and die or get up. Many people have had a hard time understanding how while in pain I could get up to do a favor for someone, or decide spontaneously to go sing, dance, or travel. Is the alternative to stay home and be miserable?

(I dare any of these people to be repeatedly cut open and bedridden for at least three months and see what coping and empowerment mechanisms they use.) But health has not been my only lesson in transformation. There were other influences that impacted my transformation processes, such as my deep connection to territories of war and peace.

One of my favorite quotes about war and hope comes from UN Canadian General Roméo Dallaire, who stayed behind in Rwanda's genocide. He states in his book *Shake Hands with the Devil* (page xviii):

> "I know there is a God because in Rwanda I shook hands with the devil. I have seen him, I have smelled him, and I have touched him. I know the devil exists and therefore I know there is a God."

It is in these moments of extreme pain that you are tested to see what you can handle and transform. War and death to me are real, perhaps because I have had them close to me most of my life. I have seen the long-term effects it has had in my community and family. Thus, I cannot look the other way when I sense pain and see injustice. I also know great humanitarians, such as Roméo Dallaire and many others, have been faced with some of humanity's worst atrocities. And like others, I have made a choice to stay, help and because of this, amid complete darkness, they found hope. They forced themselves to create hope when others could not. When the entire world looked away, Dallaire faced this nightmare and was the only light.

But why is this important to me as a leader and as a human? My parents were born in a place and a culture that has been at war with itself for most of its existence—El Salvador. Violence in this place should come as no surprise to anyone. It is the peace that troubles people and creates disbelief about people's true intentions. Furthermore, I find that most have become cynics to the point of disbelief that perhaps there is hope for a peaceful, productive life, and cultural transformation. (Note: I do not want to homogenize the El Salvador image to be solely violence because there is a lot of beauty to El Salvador, but I need to share my lessons from war and peace.)

I cannot join in the pessimism because from all this tragedy I learned some of the most valuable traits of survival and transformation for success. You do not give up because of death, war, or disaster. You get right back up. You develop a conscience to support others, and you lead— and you lead with a vengeance! You do not stay down. You get up, fight back, or find a solution. You can simultaneously be silent but firm in your beliefs, strategize, seek help, connect with others, revolutionize thoughts, perform actions, and flee if necessary to survive. Leave everything you have ever known to reach your dreams, but you do not give up! You carry your culture, beliefs, traditions, family, providing a helping hand and your love for who you are to keep moving forward.

All these elements are real and part of my spirit and history, but as a leader, I chose peace with active, conscious, social responsibility, even though war has caused disasters in the lives, bloodlines, and histories of many people I know and love. I have heard stories of running away, resiliency, negotiation for someone's life, the beauty and celebration of our food, music, and humor. Raised in the US and living half of my life in El Salvador, I knew the effects of war, classism, racism, sexism, immigration, refugees, and lack of education. I experienced the impact of those who immigrated abroad and those who returned to their home country. These stories make part of my cultural DNA memory.

Yes, I knew war. I understood post-traumatic stress disorder (PTSD) when I was eight years old. I understood the effects of evil and the need to survive and how important it was for us to be a helping hand as my parents had taught me. What I couldn't wrap my thoughts around was the idea why any leader, government, employer, family man, and friend would ever want to hurt anyone, degrade their people and work force. It never made sense. It never will to me. There must be more than money, power, and greed! So, leading with purpose, passion, and a conscience became my way to connect and grow. Especially challenging the status quo and always looking for alternatives and innovations to deal with in any given situation, is what I look for in my work and daily life.

Lead with peace or lead with war? I have both in me, but I prefer a combination of peace, strength, commitment, and to speak up for my rights and those of others. It is also important to hold your silence. I will not lie—it takes almost every fiber in my body to operate from a conscious place, regardless of what issues or conflicts arise. But having awareness, and full consciousness of my feelings, emotions, and reactions is an integral part of leading a better life.

SELF-EVALUATION/REALITY CHECK

Great! I was officially in business! I was no longer a freelancer or had to split my time between jobs. I could take care of my health and still have economic stability for myself and others without worrying about a boss and a regular schedule. To this day, it's hard to accept that I was not well. I was destroyed, and I was not making the best decisions, but I had to keep telling myself I was fine to continue forward, or it would have all collapsed. At times, people who knew nothing about me or my struggles judged me as secretive, or perhaps that I was not speaking up and purposely pushed my buttons, or conspired around me because they wanted a response from me that fit their mold.

The fact was, I could not even respond, and I had to pick my battles so as not to crumble under pressure. At the peak of my work season, when those who were supposed to support me would leave me hanging, I would have to work 23 hours daily because someone deleted my entire database. (Whether on purpose or not, I will never know, but things like this happened.) At the same time, I had clients I had to honor, and all the while, I would be working from bed between medications capturing the minutes of lucid thought and hiring and training a new team virtually. The goal: Keep going—failure was never an option! Eventually, we made it happen!

I had to recognize that out of my needing to help others and wanting to look at the good in people while trying to maintain a "normal life," that is, keep my family, friends, business associates, and relationships around, I had lost the ability to see that not everyone was going to be looking out for me or be authentic. I had lost my radar of who I could trust. I had lost my voice, assertiveness, and empowerment. Me, the one who always spoke up for herself and others. I could not even look at myself in the mirror. I wanted to save my life, business, finances, and dreams and bring everyone along for the ride including Latinos I mentored, family, friends, and clients. I thought they had my back. I thought I could make it work and find solutions. Sadly, sometimes the only solution was to stand my ground and let them go. I learned to make the tough decisions, no matter how much it would hurt me.

My clients, who were often from affluent Caucasian backgrounds, had no clue how much they were hurting and belittling me. (Or maybe they did?) Not everyone was like this, but there were many who crushed my soul and often questioned my credentials when I wanted to renegotiate terms. I was often shut down before starting. Funny, after working so many years advocating for women's rights, farm worker's rights, and immigrants' rights, I found myself feeling like I needed an advocate, but I had no one. Worst of all, I had lost myself. All I could do was solve the immediate, small tasks and strategize for the future, but often, when all was said and done, I would just cry and pray for it to all be over. In my heart, I knew I was trying my best and only had to trust that God would one day show me the path as to why I was going through all this negativity.

I remember driving to work one winter morning on I-80 toward Sacramento on my mission to help others. I realized that I felt as if I were having an out-of-body experience. That day marked a stage in my life where at least 80 percent of my days it would feel as if my spirit had left my body. I had to remind myself to stay present because I felt gone. You know—one foot here and one in the afterlife.

I was someone who always trusted her instincts, ability to be quick, strategic—using my mind to its fullest potential and my gut instinct. I did not know what to do. I was not fully myself anymore, and, worst of all, I could not let the world know because it felt like the world would not be as kind, loving, and supportive as I thought it should be. I was right, but either way, I found a way each time that someone hurt me to let it go! I had to live life as if it was my last day and make it count.

I finally learned the lesson of transformation, the third time that death came knocking. It was a complete surprise because I was feeling healthy. I took this last blow as a sign of my body telling me that even though I was healthier,—had I learned the lesson? Oddly enough, I had a point a reference and a plan. Regardless if I made it or not, I had structures, the right support system, and processes in place for my life and business that would make an easy transition for me and those who needed to continue to work and lead on my behalf.

CONCLUSION—ALWAYS UPLIFT YOUR SPIRIT

The constants in life are change, turmoil, success, peace, and good times in rotation. At each stage, learn that life is teaching you or passing you to the next level. Moreover, are you keeping a positive outlook despite the challenges? What have you learned from yourself and others who have faced adversity and evolved? Those who did not crumble under the pressure, what steps did they take? Are you there now? What will be your grounding power to keep you firm, alive, strong, and ready to keep moving forward to lead?

As you pass through the stage of leading through a transformational challenge, consider these thoughts.

1. Stay present to find your mission to influence change.

2. Self-evaluate and lead with example. Accept your mistakes.

3. Empower by showing it can be done for yourself! Then lead from there, because although many might not agree, they cannot argue that it cannot be done. You have shown the way.

4. Transform nothing into something, particularly when you have lost.

5. Advocate and have the strength to be silent and the courage to speak up.

6. Women, young and old, please trust your body; it knows when something is wrong. It does not require you to be a healthcare professional. Visit my Webpage at www.roxanadamas.soy to learn about PCOS, health advocacy, rebalance, and empowerment.

The benevolent transformation of the body and the soul to be a "mindful leader" does not come quickly, and it is not for the faint of heart. Question every area of life, and do it with a smile. Look around at most of the people who are successful, who are pioneers, and who started their overall life wealth from nothing. These people, these leaders, almost never had it easy. You are called. You feel it. You know when it is your time to take charge and lead in any area of life. Most importantly, you know when it is time for you to transform and to build yourself up to thrive!

ROXANA DAMAS, MBA

Roxana Damas, with over 15 years of consulting locally, nationally and internationally, is the founder and CEO of **RGD Enterprises Inc.,** the parent corporation for three businesses: *RD Consulting & Translations (RDCT)*, *Diversity RD Global,* and *Roxana Damas Music & Productions.*

RD Consulting & Translations bridges the gap in technology and business to Latino and other underserved communities. *Diversity RD Global* is a consulting firm specializing in all forms of diversity work, public affairs, strategic development and corporate social responsibility projects. *Roxana Damas Music & Productions*, the original business that she began at 17, is now a family business that includes music, entertainment, publishing, event productions and as a singer a platform/instrument for her message.

Damas is committed to the betterment of small businesses, non-profits, corporate social responsibility, and financial empowerment, by bridging the digital divide, language access, and community engagement projects. Her unique blend of training and work experience in the fields of business administration, public and international relations, immigration, public policy, human rights, social services, gender issues, educational programs, and violence prevention are assets in creating business innovation, start-ups, and uniquely designed new projects.

Roxana is a popular public speaker and frequent co-host of a variety of events, radio, and TV shows. Roxana had a successful season as a co-host of a financial empowerment segment on Mundo Fox & TV Estrella Northern CA. She has appeared on Buenos Dias Sacramento through Univision, Sacramento. She appears on a regular basis on La Radio 1010 and reaches over 200,000 individuals nationwide. Roxana and her team are ready to launch the Empodérate online portal project and RebeLatina Fest 2017. Both projects have a foundation in Roxana's background in community advocacy, empowerment, and leadership and are seeking to reach the Latino and underserved communities of color to improve their economic, professional, and business development. Most recent, Damas was selected as a 2016/17 champion of **Women Economic Empowerment** in conjunction with the United Nations. She will use her experience to develop partnerships, allies and platforms for discussions, internationally, during her year of service.

Roxana's dedication and vision are that her business and civic efforts will support individual and community transformations. As a result of years of investing in socially responsible work, she has started the non-profit Alquimia Global to help those most in need through a non-profit humanitarian model.

MOTHERHOOD: FROM DARKNESS TO LIGHT

THAT MOMENT

So we land in Denver for yet another weekend gateway on December 2012.

I began to feel a little strange prior to the trip, but in my head there was no time to slow down. I dismissed all the signs or perhaps I just did not want to believe my 24th birthday weekend celebration, less than a month prior, had left me a little present behind. Wanting peace of mind, I bought a pregnancy test and planned to take it right before boarding the plane. That morning, like every other morning, we left rushing to catch the plane right before takeoff. My girls and I arrived in Denver just in time for brunch, so I decided to just enjoy the Thursday, and cheers with mimosas for our time together and new adventures to come. Throughout the day I thought about the pregnancy test I had in my purse, but remembered reading somewhere on the internet that the morning pee is the best pee so I decided to push it back until the next morning. As the night progressed, we headed to the bars and I remembered having this feeling inside telling me I should only have two beers. Little did I know that it was the last night I would be out with my friends without a real care in the world other than when our next adventure would be.

It's Friday morning, there's no more putting it off, time to face the truth. This is where the feeling of holy shit this could change everything runs through my body. This is that moment in time that defines what the rest of my life will stand for. Alright, let's do it. Let's find out. The thoughts that are running in my head are so conflicting. There is only two ways this could go. I can no longer take the uncertainty. I go ahead and take the test, I walk out of the restroom and I am shaking. I pace back and forth, holding the pregnancy test in my hand and begging someone to come read the results. I don't think I had the courage to take the answer first. I wanted it filtered through someone's eyes so perhaps maybe they can see what I am terrified of knowing. Then my friend says the words that changed my life forever, "You're pregnant." In shock I responded "Shut up, whatever, you're lying, stop messing with me, it's cool, I already know, I mean it's going to be okay." My friends were scattered in the living room not really knowing what to do or say. It just so happens that, Laura, the comforting "mom" type friend with the best words and hugs did not make this particular trip. We all just stood there in silence. I feel as even the music in the background mellowed down and everything just stood still for what felt like an eternity. In my head I went from what's the worst that can happen straight to oh. shit. what. the. fuck. just. happened. I thought of Jenni Rivera right away, and I said to myself, "If she is doing it with 5 kids, on her own, after everything she's been through, killing it, still positive, with so much faith in God, successful, and influential…I think Ima be alright."

I remember feeling love, fear, excitement, shame, joy, bitterness, all at the same exact moment.

Thank God.

I wanted to believe that even though I did not know the answers or what to feel, I knew the Universe placed the army of divine souls together just for me to receive such news. Not only people, but I remember feeling like I was exactly where I was supposed to be at that precise moment in time.

I did the only thing I knew how to do. I called my people up to share this so that I did not have to hold this alone, I wanted to feel supported, and most importantly I wanted them to keep me from freaking out. I spread the news like a slow flame to my closest circle. I guess I was owning it and allowing myself to feel all the feelings. All of them without holding back; how else do you react to this other than cry, laugh, scream, smile, shit your pants, and close your eyes just to get the smallest glimpse of faith? I quickly called my sister Dora during a crying scene so it freaked her out. Her first thought was that someone had died or something tragic happened, she's a bit of a worrier. I calmed my breath and said well yes (the old me) but not really more like the opposite. I am pregnant, the first reaction was something along the lines of her being shocked that I was even having sex.

It was time to let the father of my child know. He worked night shift so I knew he'd be asleep during the day so I had to attempt the call a few times. I was kind of glad every time he didn't answer. He called back, I told him the news and there was a long awkward silence. I guess he was in total disbelief too. We really didn't have many words, it was a total state of shock. I believe the following series of events it was how God was assuring me that not only will I be fine, but it will be Divine. During lunch the waitress, who now I know was my Guardian Angel in disguise, showed up in the most graceful way to remind me of my strength and that I was being taken care of. We saw a big chalkboard with the words "Before I die I want to..." and I wrote the word "Complete." We then went to an art show and as much as I wanted to enjoy and feel confident that everything was okay, I found a little corner in the back and just cried my eyes out. The next day we went skiing, it was my first time so I was not going to miss out. I looked it up, my baby was about the size of a blueberry, and in fact we started calling her Booberry since her dad's nickname is Boo. She would be fine. I remember going up on the lift overlooking the snow, just her and I, where I had my first conversation with her. As I was crying, I told her that I could not wait to show her how beautiful the world is and that I already felt so much love for her. It all still seemed a little surreal, I was in this magical city with the most loving beautiful people. I felt as if I was floating on the outside and at the same time crumbling down on the inside. We headed back home on the same Sunday the news broke about Jenni Rivera's accident. I could not stop thinking of how ironic that she was the first person I thought of as inspiration and who I've always looked up could now be gone, it was heartbreaking. It was however somehow a relief that because I was away I did not have to face my parents with the news. I was so scared. They've never even met a boyfriend of mine, now I got to tell them I'm pregnant. What are they going to think of me? In our Mexican culture, we do not talk about sex until it is too late.

THE JOURNEY

Before the day that changed my life, I was pretty much your average young girl lost in the world. I was tirelessly looking for something external to make me happy. Life on social media looked pretty great, but deep inside I was fighting years of depression and heartbreak. I thought that happiness was something we searched for and perhaps it would come in the form of my next trip, maybe a boyfriend, yet another shopping trip, or possibly I would find it the next time I went out. This was a never ending cycle and eventually I ended up in the same spot, filling my mind and life with activities or things to distract me from my reality. That Friday morning in Denver made me think so much and question every decision in my life that lead me that very moment. I felt terrified, doubtful, and actually a little mad at life. But now I had to find the courage to tell my parents. My Mom's response was comforting. She said something inappropriate and funny, and quickly was full of joy and gave me a hug. I believe I waited another week before telling El Jefe. I invited my Dad to walk the dogs, I waited until we were halfway through our route. I figured half of the walk I could enjoy it as just his daughter who stresses him out and the other half as the daughter who was going to stress him even more. I knew what was coming, the 21 questions and like always I needed to be quick with my responses. He asked why and if I didn't know about protection. I remember him asking if the guy was my boyfriend or I thought he was my boyfriend (that one hurt), and he finished with "vas ser niño o niño?" We are three girls in the family, I feel as though he always wanted a boy around. I smiled because that was his way of showing his excitement and in that moment I knew we were going to still be cool and I could count on my family for anything.

Oh, Motherhood. The most beautiful and scariest experience that could have ever happened to me. The pregnancy was a breeze and I felt beautiful inside and out. So like my dad guessed, the father of my child and I were not actually together. We didn't know what to make of it, we talked and said it was only fair since we had no idea if we even liked each other, to try it for our unborn child. This was going to be my first boyfriend, I hated that it had to be under these circumstances. It didn't really feel real, like if we had to and it was forced because it was. At one point I made us have the talk about what it was and what it wasn't. I felt really alone the whole 9 months, I always knew deep down inside I was going to be a single mom. I kept telling him that I really hope things would change once she arrives. The months flew by with both excitement to this new addition and uncertainty of what our life will look like. I did find a beautiful escape with prenatal yoga where I did not feel so alone and was able to connect with a living being inside of me. Around this time, Jenni Rivera's autobiography was released. I feel like her words held me, filled me with hope, and reminded me that it would not be the end of the world. I too can do this.

It all happened so fast, I realized I didn't have a place to live and staying with my roommate was probably not the best option. My sister suggested that I buy a house and without really thinking things just kind of happened. Thank you God, for always providing. I did not take in consideration how the father would take this, I just knew I had to start making moves for the future. The first week of August in 2013, I felt like I was forced to become an adult at 24. I closed on my house on Monday, got the keys on Tuesday, had my friends help me clean and move everything and that night as I was feeling contractions. I would stop from directing where I wanted the couch, to feel a contraction and then pose for a picture. We headed to the hospital just in time for my partner in all of this to get off from work and meet me and my little sister there. It still seemed unreal to me. Literally 8 hours later and with just a few little scares, on that beautiful Wednesday morning, I was holding the love of my life in my arms. I felt elevated and blissful and full of instant love. She was beautiful, she was perfect, and she already meant the world to me. Jaylah Lari Edwards. I always knew her name would be Jaylah, I would practice writing it during meetings at work. I got the name from Jenni Rivera's granddaughter, I loved it ever since I first heard it on her TV show. I figured it would be fair if her dad picked the middle name. I really would have loved the names Rose or Love. I surrendered to his choice after he announced her middle name during the baby shower in honor of his little sister who he is really close to.

The elevated blissful state might have lasted 3 days. Once we left the hospital and arrived to a new home with this new life, I did not know what to do with the new me. I was determined to breastfeed at whatever cost. I was drained and sleep deprived and was barely functioning. I felt alone, afraid, paranoid, scared and yet full of this newfound feeling of love that I had never experienced before. I was literally mad at the world that I had to do all of this alone. I was very angry and resentful that everything fell on the woman even though it was just her and I at the house. Looking back, I can only imagine all the ugly things I was telling her dad which only made him come around less and less. It was horrible. I wanted to run away but literally could not. A day would pass and it seemed like a week. My family would come around to try to help but we were all just trying to figure it out. This is the first baby in the family, and things have changed since the last baby. I also read too many articles online on different parenting styles as I was trying to figure out my own. I do remember my sister telling me that I was dealing with postpartum depression and I got mad. How dare she tell someone who doesn't even know the last time she showered that she has a condition? My life had been turned upside down, and as strong willed and determined to have things my way, I just wanted things to be quiet so I could get some rest to recover. Jaylah was a colic baby and it took me a few months to figure out that eating dairy was also causing her stomach to be upset. All this caused her to cry... to cry a lot and was the reason why I was going crazy. This also brought self-guilt. I felt I was causing all this pain to my baby and she had no say in it. It was just not a good picture all around. I remember one night in particular early on, where I was just miserable. It was the middle of the night and I could no longer go on. I had a crying baby on my lap and I just broke down crying and prayed "God, this is too much. I cannot. Help me." It felt like a breath of comfort instantly embraced me. That moment kept me going.

The three months of maternity leave were over and I was low-key a little relieved. Finally I could have a lunch without interruption. The drive to work was just me, my thoughts and my music. It was what I knew and definitely an escape from my new reality. I worked in radio so my job was somewhat fun. There was always events happening. I was stuck in the constant battle between wanting to go to all of them and having to care for my child. This was also my livelihood which made it hard. It was an intense period of time where I would drive to work rushed, be stressed out at work and having to pump every 3 hours (sometimes even at my desk), drive home while pumping with a cover up because in my head I only wanted her breastfed. I was literally killing myself, and felt this cannot be real life. How much can one person handle?

THE DISCOVERY

Oh that life can get old really quick. The non-stop hustle and bustle and not ever slowing down. The resistance for a new way was real. I kept seeing the signs, my friend would showed up with a book, and invited me to do the 40 day meditation journey with her. My ego once again resisting change kept screaming, "I barely have time to sleep, how the fuck am I going to meditate? These girls don't know my life. Nobody lives what I live, nobody feels what I feel, nobody is there day in and day out. I'm so alone in this world left to figure it all out." I believe there comes a point during the madness that the only way out is to believe that this does not have to be the way. I do have to acknowledge that as bad as all this sounds I did have the help and support of my family. They never did leave my side, no matter how mean I got. I do remember squeezing in my concert nights, I even managed to escape to NY for Romeo Santos' first sold out night at the Yankee Stadium with two of my best friends thanks to my sister for always having my back.

Surrender was the word. Turning it over to God, because this old way of just trusting on my own understanding and ability was not really working out for us. I started to invite God in and just started seeing things through the eyes of Love again. I think the biggest game changer was Gratitude. I started noticing all the blessings in my life and love and support around me. My family, my Mom and my Dad their support and never ending worry for not just me but for their baby Jaylah. My little sister Katy, who would randomly show up with food to hang out with us and my older sister moved in to keep us company. The amount of Love and Light Jaylah brought to our family, it is indescribable. My favorite cousin Dani, who not only came within the first weeks of Jaylah's life to help me but also offered an escape to California to stay with her and feel safe and held. My friends who never left my side, as much as their lives were changing, I never felt abandoned and I knew I can pour out my heart to either one of them at any time. And yes, my job was at times stressful but I worked with the best coworkers who were also my friends that cared about my well-being and were also emotionally involved in my story. I had a job. I had a house. I have a baby. I am healthy. She is healthy. I am richer than I actually thought. Wow, all of this could be way worse. And it is not, and for that I am grateful.

The relationship between her father and I was a bit strange. I quickly learned that my way of confronting a problem was very different than his, but for some reason did not bother to consider a different approach. We had known each other 6 months prior to this, we literally did not know each other. We had to learn about each other under the most difficult circumstances. When he would come see his daughter, all I wanted to do was unleash this anger and frustration that was screaming to come out. I know I have a lethal tongue, and words are a powerful weapon that can be used to either create or destroy. The moment in which I was finally able to see things different was right after a Beyoncé concert in Philly, the next morning my friend Grecia and I drove to the Hamptons to attend a Gabby Bernstein workshop. Gabby Bernstein is a spiritual teacher, author, and life coach whose work had been appearing in my life since my pregnancy. My Tia Nelly handed me her first book "Add more ~Ing to your life" which I was not ready for at the time. Shortly after Jaylah's birth Grecia came to my house with another of her books, "May Cause Miracles" which I also ignored. I then found myself on her website and everything just made sense, I was finally able to receive the message. The lesson of that day by the beach was my favorite Dr. Wayne Dyer quote, "Change the way you look at things, the things you look at change." Oh wow, duh. I was not letting him be the father he knew or wanted to be, I was only projecting all these ideas of what I thought a father should be. That same day a lady shared something with me that really shifted me as I shared with her my experience as a single mom and the guilt I felt for wanting to do my own thing and having to do it all at home. She said the words "When I am serving and attending my children; that is when I feel the closest to God." Wow. That changed it for me, what an honor to experience something as joyful as motherhood. This is one of those reminders I keep in my back pocket when my energy is low, my body is tired, and I do everything to avoid the next bath, the meal, the reading the book, all of it. I started to tap into the delight of what it means to be a mom. It is incredible how a powerful a simple shift in the mind can really play a part of the life we live.

PURPOSE

What does it mean to live a life with purpose? The beauty of that answer is that it is different to everyone. Like the beautiful Pablo Picasso quote, "The meaning of life is to find your gift. The purpose of life is to give it away." As I was going through the madness I always heard a voice inside of me assuring me that I am living this for a reason, I have to be a voice for all the others that are going through or have been in my situation. I think being in radio made me see that reality much closer than it was. I always knew I wanted a mic in my hand, I was just learning the lessons of what I would actually say. The year 2016 was the most transformational of my life. I looked within, I started tuning out and tuning in to the power inside of me. I started to take time for myself and stop people pleasing and only do the things that felt right and served my highest self. I let go of guys that did not see what I was finally discovering about my true self. It has been a process, because as soon as the soul makes an advancement the mind wants to protect you and trick you into thinking that it is safer not to change. It takes a lot of self-assessment, reevaluating, and most of all being truly raw and authentic to yourself. I believe we all have the power to start seeing life in this way, what is required is the desire AND the courage to change. And what is needed to actually make a shift is being easy on oneself and forgiving ourselves as much as needed. It is a never ending life journey. We must embrace it as such.

I don't know if it is a particular moment or if it is a series of events that lead you to that moment where it clicks. I feel like it could be either or both. Whatever it is, it is magical. It is where you feel supported, guided, and directed beyond your understanding or control. It is faith at its' finest. And it literally moves mountains. It moves you, it breaks you, and fills you with this energy that is indescribable. The scariest part is showing up. Fear will always find a way to creep back in, and I think the secret here is not fighting it, instead we can just acknowledge it and recognize it as is and remember in that moment to choose Love.

I don't think anyone could have put it better than Marianne Williamson on Return to Love when she stated, "Our deepest fear is not that we are inadequate. Our deepest fear is that we are powerful beyond measure. It is our light, not our darkness that most frightens us. We ask ourselves, who am I to be brilliant, gorgeous, talented, and fabulous? Actually, who are you *not* to be? You are a child of God. You playing small does not serve the world. There is nothing enlightened about shrinking so that other people won't feel insecure around you. We are all meant to shine, as children do. We were born to make manifest the glory of God that is within us. It's not just in some of us; it's in everyone. And as we let our own light shine, we unconsciously give other people permission to do the same. As we are liberated from our own fear, our presence automatically liberates others."

That has got to be one of the realest quotes ever. It is just one of those reminders that shake you from having any moment of self-doubt, self-sabotage, or anything that is really not serving any of us. That is what we are here to do, to create the magic in our souls and by doing so we invite others to do the same. I believe there is a big paradigm shift happening, and it is truly an honor and a big responsibility to own our part in it and SHOW UP.

Showing up as a soul, as a woman, as a mother, as a daughter, as a sister, as a friend, and as all the other labels that we have taken on but know that the most important of them all as YOUR spirit. It is vital that your cup is full, so full that is overflowing, then and only then can you actually serve others. Please know that self-love and self-care are not selfish, they are necessary and crucial for our well-being. It is my vision and my mission to share all this knowledge and wisdom that I have recollected on this journey which is why I created MorenaMagic, a purpose-driven company focused on empowering women and their families through the art of healing, self-love, and unity. There is a lot of suffering in this world, and we are living in a time where we are really divided. THE TIME IS NOW. And we must take action this very moment. First of all knowing ourselves, our pain, our grief, our joy, what makes us angry, what makes us happy and not judging any of it. Just owning it and working through all the bad to let more good in.

Oh and the magic will unfold. As you take one step in your devotion, the Universe will take ten. As you pray and ask for the signs, the signs will appear and they will keep showing up until you are able to see and receive. Stepping into my power has been the biggest challenge of this year. But I refuse to keep replaying the same movie scene. I am here to break barriers and to do what scares me the most, which also makes me feel the most alive. Everything is aligning and it is so divine. As Gabby

Bernstein says, "Just as I surrender and let go, something shows up to teach me to surrender some more." Life is meant to be lived, to be felt, to be made love to and our job is merely to remove all the blocks both internally and externally that are keeping us from all those great feelings. I strongly believe we are here to simply remind one another of what we already know. And like a good cup of cafecito, it always better when shared with someone else.

Now every time I look into my daughter's eyes; I see my greatest teacher. She is the reason I am on this path. She chose me, and God chose the perfect moment. Everything is aligning and it can be overwhelming and scary at times. I know I am here for something greater than myself. Looking back on the dates, she was actually conceived on 11/11 and 4 years later on 11/11 again the name of my company came to me. She is my #MorenaMagic. I have to be very mindful to not let all this Magic keep me from the reason I am doing it; for her. I am raising my child first and foremost, although it does take a village, I want to be present and conscious every possible moment. I also want to show her that anything is possible. That just because something unexpected happens that does not mean you stop dreaming. *Al contrario*, you keep dreaming and bigger. This is for us. We are meant to live this life. Nobody said it was going to be easy, but we can however enjoy this beautiful ride we call Life.

JENNIFER IBARRA

Jennifer Ibarra is a Soul Coach, Author, and TV Host who stands for Love and Liberation. She is the Founder and CEO of MorenaMagic, a purpose-driven company focused on empowering women of color and their families through the art of healing, self-love and unity. Jennifer Ibarra is also a certified Isadora Tantra Coach, Quantum-Touch Level 1 and Spirit Junkie Level 1 healer and coach. Jennifer's professional background comes from Spanish broadcasting where she spent six years with Univision. Jennifer currently works for the Blue Zones Project in Fort Worth, Texas—a community-led well-being initiative. She is a single mom of a 3 year-old daughter who ignited her passion and fire to help women see the divine light and power within. Visit MorenaMagic.com to learn more.

ABOUT THE COVER ARTIST: PHEPHE ROSE

"When creating with purpose, you will become an inspiration to others. Use your gift to inspire, and the world will never stop creating." —Phephe Rose

We all learn to hold a crayon before we ever learn how to hold a pencil. Blank pieces of paper are put in front of us and we scribble over and over again with a remarkable sense of imagination and creativity at such a young age. However, too often as we grow older, we are discouraged from the arts from various pressures or lack or resources, and we never get to cultivate our talent. Phephe Rose was blessed to have never stopped creating and believes our next generations shouldn't have to either.

Phephe Rose is a half Mexican and half Filipino Artist, Designer, Speaker and Advocate for the creative arts. She is passionate about inspiring creativity in our next generation and guiding creatives to turn their hobby into a professional brand.

Growing up in multicultural household, Phephe loved to spend hours drawing. She was fortunate enough to have parents and a grandmother who supported her artistic interests. She took rec center art classes, was a visual arts major through SCPA at Chula Vista High School, and holds a Bachelor of Architecture from the University of Southern California.

Phephe leaped into entrepreneurship and gained an *experiential degree* in business, with one of her many ventures reaching 6 figures in revenue in just under 6 months. With her passion to create, she combined her artistic skills and business knowledge, to create her company, **Phephe Rose Studio**. Her favorite medium is watercolor. She designs and illustrates for nonfiction and children's literature, and also loves to design imaginative children's bedrooms. She consults other creatives and companies on visual branding.

When Phephe is not in her studio creating, you can find her in the classroom inspiring children or giving workshops and speeches on following your passion with purpose. Her latest project is ***Adventures of Mila***— a series of children's illustrations and stories capturing the adventures of the lovable character, Mila Bunny. ***Adventures of Mila*** inspires and teaches children about the adventures of curiosity, exploration and new cultures as Mila travels across the world in a once in a bunnytime experience.

Phephe also has a soft spot for uplifting and encouraging young Latinas who want to follow a creative career, and she occasionally mentors high school students in the So Cal area.

You can connect with Phephe at PhepheRose.com, on social media at @ phepherose or by email at phephe@phepherose.com. Go to PhepheRose. com/WhyDoIInspire to download her "Why Do I Inspire?" mantra and join the movement to inspire others.

Made in the USA
Middletown, DE
04 February 2024

49089178R00087